THE POLISH AUGUST

THE POLISH AUGUST

Documents from the Beginnings of the Polish Workers' Rebellion
Gdansk · August, 1980

Edited by Oliver MacDonald

ZP

ZTANGI PRESS
SAN FRANCISCO

The contents of this book, except the foreword, the update of the chronicle and the afterword, originally appeared in Vol. 4, Nos. 1-3, of *Labour Focus on Eastern Europe*, Box 23, 136 Kingland High St., London E8.

This North American Edition published not-for-profit by Ztangi Press, Suite 832, 55 Sutter St., San Francisco, CA. 94104.

CONTENTS

FOREWARD

These documents from Poland first appeared in a special Polish issue of **Labour Focus on Eastern Europe** (Vol. 4, Nos. 1-3), a journal published in London which is devoted to reporting on and rallying support for dissidents. Some of this material was translated from the Polish especially for **Labour Focus** and the remainder comes by way of translations from the French **L'Alternative**, a bulletin publishing similar material on the continent. All of it has been authenticated with the original.

We are making this material available for the first time on this side of the Atlantic to help inform the general public of the early history and activity of Solidarity (Solidarność in Polish). A clear understanding of the tremendous upheaval in Poland is absolutely essential for a proper international defense and support of these developments.

We earnestly invite all correspondence to further this project.

i INTRODUCTION

A CHRONICLE OF THE WORKERS' SOLIDARITY

—By Oliver MacDonald
Editor of Labour Focus

Trying to Buy Some Authority, July 1st—16th.

As in 1970 and 1976 it began this time with a price increase. But while in the past the price increase was to tackle the government's economic problems, this time the price increase was to show that the government had the authority to increase prices. As the strikes spread and the workers were given larger and larger cash deals the government's saving from the price increase was wiped out. But what the government wanted above all was to show the world that it had the political authority and the nerve—Polish workers would have said the cheek—to raise meat prices. And it was prepared to pay almost any amount of compensation to workers to buy that political authority.

So during the first fortnight of July the government stuck to its price increase, the workers struck, elected leaders, raised economic demands. Government and management paid to settle the strikes without cutting meat prices. In this way Gierek's phoney economic measures paved the way for the future political crisis.

Lublin: A Prologue taken as an Epilogue.

Between 16 July and 19 July, the workers of Lublin downed tools in a general strike, raising sharp economic demands including one calling for family benefits equal to those of the militia. The regime responded with a mixture of hints of military action and an offer to pay most of the money. A commission under Deputy Premier Jagielski negotiated a deal and the workers went back to work.

The elated government thought that the strike movement would peter out. They evidently imagined that if they could handle such a major problem as the Lublin general strike, they could handle anything. But they had ignored the speed, organization, unity and political edge in the Lublin strike. It was to be a foretaste of things to come.

From Economic to Political Action. July 19th—August 14th.

The workers' strikes continued to roll through Poland during the following month, and the small groups of organized political activists around the KOR (Polish initials of the Workers Defense Committee) collected and spread news of the strikes. Workers in different parts of the country began to realize that they were part of a much wider, national movement, not isolated.

After organizing a successful strike for more money, the workers' mood was not one of gratefulness and contentment. They saw the source of their problem as a bungling, dictatorial and corrupt government. The strike victories gave new confidence to struggle for more than just a wage increase that could be eroded by inflation later on.

THE WORKERS STRIKE BACK

Sectional Action or Class Action? Gdansk, August 14th—17th.

The Gdansk strike began in the Lenin Shipyard on 14 August and immediately began to spread. The spark had been the sacking of Mrs. Walentynowicz, a veteran militant in the Yard, but the workers had also raised economic demands. The workers' leaders negotiated a deal on the economic demands and voted to recommend a return to work. But the mass meeting at the yard threw the deal out.

The rank-and-file workers in the yard had received appeals from busmen not to abandon the weaker sections of workers, but to stay united till the demands of all the workers had been won. The Lenin workers had responded to their appeal. Solidarity and class action were the order of the day.

On 17 August the strike leaders from all the striking work places in the Gdansk-Gdynia-Sopot area met and took two decisive, historic steps: they drew up 21 demands, the most important of which called for the right to strike and the right to form an independent, self-managed trade union. Secondly, they created a class organization to lead the struggle for the 21 demands, the Inter-factory Strike Committee, known by its Polish initials as MKS. The workers' devastating answer to the government's meat price insult of 1 July was on the move.

The United Workers' Party Against the United Workers, August 18th—30th.

During the course of the struggle hundreds of factories and work places from the entire region struck and joined the MKS. Delegates were elected and democratic decisions taken on many aspects of the people's social life, from keeping the coastal trains running to keeping booze out of the striking work-places. The industrial workers in their mass meetings exercised effective control over all important decisions—the very opposite of the system that had brought Poland's economy to the brink of catastrophe.

Totally out of touch with the real opinions of the mass of working people, the Gierek group tried to mobilize support for a campaign against the 'counter-revolutionary, anti-socialist' demands of the Gdansk strikers for independent trade unions. They also tried to undermine and destroy the supposedly 'counter-revolutionary' MKS, attempting to entice individual factories into separate negotiations with the government.

The government campaign got off to a disastrous start with Gierek's TV appeal for a return to work. The following day the strikes spread further. Szczecin is out and the movement is beginning in Wroclaw as well. Things get still worse as the government negotiating commission in Gdansk is unable to get any section of workers to go back to work in defiance of the MKS. Meanwhile peasants, students and intellectuals are rallying to the support of the strike movement, and the base of the Polish United Workers' Party (the official name of the CP) has either deserted to the 'counter-revolution' in the case of the strike areas, or is pushing for an agreement with the MKS and sweeping changes in the Party.

The Party leadership began to split within a week, the confrontationist circle around Gierek were put in a minority and on Sunday, 24 August Gierek's right-hand man, Prime Minister Babiuch, was ousted from power. Gierek was forced to make a public self-criticism, and two Party leaders sacked in February 1980 for advocating economic reform were brought back into the leadership. At the same time the Party leaders backed down and agreed to negotiate with the MKS.

During the week from 24 August to 30 August, the regime was fighting to avoid at all costs having to allow workers to have their own unions, and at the same time trying to contain and then end the strike. It tried to whip up popular resentment against the economic effects of the strike, but with no success. It televised an appeal by Cardinal Wyszynski urging 'moderation' upon the strikers (in comparison with their needs and desires, the workers' 21 demands were indeed ultra-moderate). Wyszynski's appeal brought no let up in the strikes. The following day the Party daily, **Trybuna Ludu** raised the threat of Soviet intervention, and on the 28th the paper ruled out independent trade unions and denounced 'anti-socialist' elements. The security forces had arrested KOR activists and an attempt was being made to suggest that dark, sinister forces were manipulating the workers.

Knockout Blow and Victory, August 28th—31st.

On Thursday 28 August the miners and engineering workers of Upper Silesia rose in their hundreds of thousands in a great strike wave that shook the Party leadership to the core. They had to choose immediately between military action against the shipyard and political capitulation to the MKS. If the drift continued there would be a national general strike at the start of the next week.

On the night of Friday the 29th, the Political Bureau apparently divided 8-5 in favor of military action against the Lenin Shipyard. Gierek was in the majority. But the security and military chiefs refused to sanction such action, on the grounds that they could not vouch for the loyalty of security forces. The minority won, the Central Committee agreed to independent trade unions, the Gdansk settlement was signed along with the settlement already agreed in Szczecin. The workers had won a gigantic victory.

ONE BIG UNION

Aftermath of the Strike: The 'Gero Syndrome'

Despite the workers' great victory, the regime still possessed some very powerful levers of power: the military armory of the Warsaw Pact, its own military apparatus, continued monopoly over the mass media, except for the foreign broadcasting stations, the skeleton of arty and state functionaries. And although the mass base of the Party—and its working-class membership—along with the rest of the population had swung over to support the strike movement, the great bulk of the workers remained very cautious. They had not been on strike, had not felt their own strength, feared the leap into the unknown involved in an all-out struggle for their rights. However much they disliked the government, they were inclined to accept its authority as a lesser evil than Soviet invasion.

But at the same time they were determined that the rights won in Gdansk should apply to them. They wanted a new deal and a clean out of the old corrupt and autocratic party bosses in their regions. And the symbol of their authority, Edward Gierek, had to go.

At this point it might have been possible for the Party leadership to re-stabilize the situation, **if** it had replaced Gierek with a radical reformer; **if** it had swiftly removed local obstacles to the emergence of new independent unions; **if** it had immediately disbanded the old unions and given the new unions a voice in the mass media; **if** it had swiftly a Party conference and swept away the old guard; **if** it had called genuine representatives of the workers together to debate and decide on a new economic plan to overcome the crisis.

But instead, what might be called the 'Gero Syndrome' took over. As in Hungary in 1956, the regime replaced the old leader with his erstwhile servant, choosing someone who could be considered 'safe' by all wings of the bureaucracy and would accordingly implement a 'safe' policy. In a system where politics has been confined to the Party oligarchy, any policy that involved actively seeking to link up with autonomous mass movement would have appeared as treason.

So the new leadership, under former police chief Kania, attempted to preserve the old guard in power (while removing some public faces at the top of the pyramid); it allowed the administrative apparatus to put every obstacle in the way of the new unions—using arrests, harassment, denial of offices and access to the media, vicious slanders of individual leaders in the media, house searches and confiscation of material. Desperate attempts were made to preserve the old official unions and to intimidate workers seeking to join the new unions. No attempt was made to swiftly convoke a party conference, and no effort was made to involve the workers' leaders in decisions on new economic measures.

So this was the 'safe' policy—one of petty harassment and provocation, requiring the workers to struggle every inch of the way to build their new organization themselves. Periodically this 'safe' policy brought the government to the brink of popular revolution, leaving the Party leadership with nothing to lean on save the threat of Soviet invasion.

Building 'Solidarity', September 1st—22nd.

On 4 September, after an agreement between the government and the leaders of 350,000 strikers in Silesia, the miners and engineering workers there return to work. At the same time the first moves are made to create independent trade union centers in Warsaw and Wroclaw as well as Gdansk. On 6 September Gierek is replaced by Kania as First Secretary of the Party.

Kania's opening speech as Party leader indicates that an attempt will be made to drive a wedge between the new unions—acceptable—and the political activists of such groups as the KOR—declared 'anti-socialist elements'. Recognizing that the crack-down on political activists was an attempt to dictate who could open their mouths and who could not, the MKS had already insisted on the release of all KOR leaders jailed during the strikes. This historic defense of the intellectuals by the workers also created a climate of free discussion by demonstrating that the workers would stamp on any attempt by the regime to repress people for speaking out.

On 15 September, after a series of bitter local struggles calling for the Gdansk agreement to be applied throughout the country, the government itself accepted this principle. The new independent union in Gdansk issued its official charter.

On 17 September, about 500 representatives of independent trade unions from all over the country met in Gdansk to start discussion on national trade union structures. On 22 September the delegates, representing 36 different independent unions, agreed to the statutes of a new national union to be called 'Solidarity' (in Polish 'Solidarność'). They agreed to the union being a Federation of 17 autonomous regional bodies with a co-ordinating commission on the national level based in Gdansk. The new union would also be structured along industrial lines.

The First Confrontation, September 22nd to October 3rd.

The regime continued its campaign of harassment during the last week of September, causing the leadership of the new union to declare on 30 September that there would be a one-hour general strike across the country unless promised wage rises were granted, the union given access to the mass media, and government harassment ended.

The authorities whip up a great campaign in the press against the strike, making it a test of strength. On the eve of the strike the Warsaw district court, empowered to register new unions, declared that 10 of the 44 points in Solidarity's statutes were unsatisfactory, especially those concerning its national character and the absence of any mention of the 'Leading Role of the Party'.

But the national strike on 3 October was a triumphant show of strength and discipline by the Solidarity membership, with short strikes taking place all over the country. The membership had not been intimidated by threats of the dire consequences of strike action. The union was claiming a membership of over 6 million (half the work force) representing some 3,500 enterprises throughout Poland.

At the same time new student associations and peasant

organizations were springing up, moving towards the creation of independent self-managed organizatons of their own.

The Second Confrontation, October 4th to November 10th.

Despite the evidence of October 3rd that the new union had consolidated its hold and could not be destroyed without bloodshed, the Party leadership continued to try desperate manoeuvres to undermine it. At the Central Committee meeting of October 4—5, despite a good deal of recrimination about the 'errors' and corruption of the past, there were only a handful of individuals seriously arguing for long-term co-operation with the new union. The argument, a very bitter one, focused on how the autonomous working-class movement could best be undermined. Some wanted a flexible, reformist manoeuvre involving a purge of the old guard and temporary co-operation with Solidarity. Others wanted to save themselves by resisting reforms. This second group emerged largely intact as a result of the meeting, though some of their leaders were dropped from the CC.

Pressure was now mounting from Poland's neighbors, especially Czechoslovakia and East Germany. The message of Solidarity was all too crisp and relevant to the workers of these countries, and the governments felt directly threatened by the Polish events. On 13 October new regulations to restrict the inflow of West Germans into East Germany came into force as part of a new cold war propaganda line. On 20 October Ceausescu of Romania accused the Polish leaders of having been too soft on 'anti-socialist elements' in the past, and on 28 October East Germany took steps to prevent Earth Germans from travelling to Poland. Similar restrictions were placed on contact between Czechs and Poles. Both the Soviet, the East German and the Czech regimes all declared unions independent of the ruling party to be 'anti-Leninist', reaffirmed the Brezhnev doctrine allowing for invasion of Warsaw Pact countries, and denounced anti-socialist and counter-revolutionary elements in Poland.

Against this background, on 24 October the Warsaw District Court wrote into the Statutes of Solidarity a clause recognizing the 'Leading role of the Party'. This formula was to be used to justify the Party leadership intervening at will in the union's internal affairs, appointing and sacking union leaders, etc. The aim of the Party leadership was to force a confrontation with Solidarity on this issue, hoping to split the union and begin a crackdown on the most clear-sighted and determined of its leaders.

The Solidarity leadership totally rejected the Warsaw Court's ruling and appealed to the Supreme Court. It had already made clear before the 24th that it would accept nothing more than a reference to the Party's leading role in the annex to the Statutes.

On 27 Ocotober a national delegate conference of Solidarity in Gdansk decided to call a strike alert for 12 November if it did not gain victory in the Supreme Court in the battle over its Statutes. Solidarity also demanded access to the media, better food supplies, the implementation of agreed wage increases, and the release of impounded printing presses.

On 30 October Party leader Kania flew unexpectedly to Moscow, returning a day later with a communiqué saying 'there had been a complete identity of views'.

On 2 November, 14 hours of negotiations with Prime Minister Pinkowski resulted in Solidarity leader Lech Walesa announcing that the union would have regular access to television and would be able to publish its own national weekly newspaper. But he refused to call off the threat of a strike on 12 November unless the Union's statutes were recognized.

On 10 November the Supreme Court met in Warsaw and declared in favor of the Solidarity position, over-ruling the lower court.

The Third Confrontation, November 19th—27th.

Government attempts to split Solidarity had been thwarted by the victories of the Union's more militant wing, out-voting those in the union urging retreat. The tremendous growth in the self-confidence and the power of the union's membership was shown in a dramatic way by the third confrontation.

The events began when a document from the Chief Prosecutor's Office was pased to members of Solidarity in Warsaw. This 14-page plan, dated 30 October, involved a round-up of key activists in Solidarity on charges of anti-socialist activity in preparation for a political trial that, it was hoped, would split the union.

When the police discovered that the document was in Solidarity's hands, a printer in Solidarity and a man in the Prosecutor's office were arrested, on 19 November.

In response, the workers in Warsaw mobilized for a battle to weaken the entire hold of the political police, demanding general strike for a series of demands against the political police. (A cut in its budget, a joint commission to investigate abuses of power by the security police, the putting on trial of those responsible for the police violence against workers in 1970 and 1976). They also, of course, demanded the immediate release of the two imprisoned men, as well as of four other political prisoners.

On 25 November Solidarity's Warsaw leadership declared a state of strike alert in Warsaw from 27 November. But already strikes had started in a number of factories. The national leadership of Solidarity in Gdansk backed the Warsaw organization but when the government released the two men detained over the issue, the Solidarity leaders managed to persuade the steel workers and other groups of workers in Warsaw to call off their general strike plans.

The workers' challenge to the security police set alarm-bells ringing in Moscow. For the Soviet leaders, not to speak of the Czechoslovak or East German regimes, the political police are the holy of holies. As the Polish Central Committee met at the beginning of December the Kremlin made great play of its concern at events in Poland, the threat of Soviet invasion was made very explicit and the Solidarity leaders were induced to declare they had no intention of taking over the government. For the moment at least, Moscow has declared its confidence in Mr. Kania.

CHRONICLE UPDATE

The Polish Central Committee Meets

Kania warned at the two day C.C. meeting in early December that "there cannot be two centers of power in the country" and as testimony to the illusion of power he had to cultivate he purged four more members of the Politburo. This action left only himself and three others (Ge. Jaruzelski, Deputy Premier Jagielski and President Jablonski) remaining of the fourteen voting members at the start of last summer's massive strikes. Coupled with the replacement of twenty of the forty-nine provincial first secretaries, these moves capped the biggest shake-up since the de-Stalinization of 1956. Further window dressing was added to mark the approaching Christmas season with the appointment of a prominent Catholic intellectual and member of the Sejm, Jerzy Ozdowski, to the post of Deputy Prime Minister.

Coincidentally to the C.C. meeting the first news reached the West that local rank and file party groups had been establishing links "horizontally" as they said to distinguish this growing network from the dominant and disreputable vertical structures of the party. In fact these links began forming as work places across the country went on strike in August. Abandoned by the party hierarchy, too busy guarding its own rear to worry about anything else, workers who were also party members (roughly one-third of the three million) had to fend for themselves and many, especially the younger ones, sided with Solidarity.

Monuments erected as fulfillment of an August demand in Gdansk and Gdynia to honor workers killed in the 1970 demonstrations were dedicated at the end of the month. The moment of truce at these ceremonies was quickly shattered by the government's unilateral decree that the free Saturdays accord could not be honored because of the worsening economic situation. But, as if it were appeasing a rambunctious child, the government granted the workers one more Saturday a month off to add to the one they already "enjoyed." And to close the year on a similar note, the Polish Supreme Court informed farmers that they had "postponed" their decision on legalizing Rural Solidarity.

The Fourth Confrontation

The New Year opened with the Saturday Question uppermost in everyone's mind. Workers saw in the government pronouncement, issued without consulting the union, a sign that the party was assuming its old role of dictating conditions to the people. The whole society therefore mobilized for implementation of the accords signed during the summer and a large majority stayed home Saturday, January 17 openly defying government pleas. The following Saturday the Ministry of the Economy itself admitted that at best only 10 percent of the workforce showed up! As Poland relaxed, Russian, East German and Czechoslovakian party officials blustered in rage.

So as to leave no doubts in the minds of those who opposed them, the people of Poland escalated their demands beyond the summer agreements and took up local issues, some of them unquestionably "political." General strikes erupted in several cities, like Lodz and Bielsko-Biala; and industrial sector strikes took place in others like Poznan where public transportation ground to a halt. In still other towns sympathy strikes in support of Rural Solidarity occurred.

Almost unnoticed in the blossoming of protest, the breadth of which far exceeded the August events, were the students who found their voice. At Lodz University five thousand students issued a four page list of demands to the Minister of Education. They then proceeded to occupy seven campus buildings until an agreement was signed recognizing their role in shaping educational policy.

At the beginning of February it was generally recognized that "there was a fire in the land" as students, factory and office workers, miners, technicians and farmers openly took their stand for a society that they controlled. Not only one commentator alluded to this as the Polish October (after the month in which the Russian Revolution erupted).

The negotiations between Solidarity and the government over the issues of free Saturdays continued throughout this volatile period. The union forced the government to first agree to one working Saturday per month and then with the massive display of support on January 24th it pushed a little more and got several hours knocked off that remaining Saturday. The fight over the number of hours wasn't quibbling, but a matter of demonstrating to the party that they could no longer renege on signed agreements with impunity.

The General Takes Over

Kania and company learned their lesson so to speak, for on February 11 General Jaruzelski took over as Prime Minister. This was an extraordinary event for Eastern Europe where no military man has ever held such a high government post. It appeared that Kania, with Jaruzelski's appointment, had effectively checkmated all his opponents. The new Prime Minister appeased the nervous Russian leadership, who respected this man who survived three regimes as Minister of Defense; his well known reluctance to use the military against the workers and his "moderate" position vis a vis their struggle added weight to Kania's attempts to isolate the party hardliners; and his popularity with the Poles, who saw him above all as an honest commuist, served as a brake on militancy in Solidarity. It was the recognition of this last point that prompted Walesa to refer to Jaruzelski's appointment as "the last chance for Poland."

The general immediately appealed to the country for "three months of uninterrupted work" — that is, a strike moratorium on the part of Solidarity. At the same time, as a sign of his government's good-will, he promised to continue the "dialogue" with Solidarity about labor law reform. To this end he put Mieczyslaw Rakowski, the editor of **Polityka**, a respected journal of Polish current events, in charge of negotiations with the union. He also appointed Mieczyslaw Jagielski, who Gierek had sent to the Lenin Shipyards to settle the strike, to take charge of the government's economic policies — the major area of Solidarity's criticism and Western banks' concern.

For its part Solidarity, seemingly at Walesa's urging, made conciliatory gestures and within days a compromise was reached at Jelenia Gora. There 250,000 workers had struck to force the resignation of corrupt local officials in what the government characterized as a forbidden 'political' strike. This wasn't the first of the "political" strikes (nor the last), but it was the biggest and the government basically gave in to the workers' demands.

Next the government turned to the striking students of Lodz whose month-long resistance had attracted twenty campuses to join them. Rather unexpectedly the students too attained a notable victory. The students won a commitment from the Ministry of Education to ban police from campuses, to grant students one-third representation on administrative boards, to abolish compulsory Russian language courses and to reduce the number of required courses in Marxism-Leninism. But most importantly, the students won an independent union.

The Farmers Unite

Ironically, the sweet smell of victory seemed confined to the cities as repeated attempts by the farmers to gain recognition of their union met stiff resistance from the state. It was clear that Kania and Jaruzelski had drawn their new line and planned to dig for a long siege. They hadn't expected that the farmers would gain the sympathy of the whole country.

The day that the General spoke about making sacrifices and returning to work, the farmers in Rzeszow, who were entering the seventh week of their occupation of the old trade union headquarters, voted to reject the Supreme Court's offer of association status and renewed their demand for full union status. Embittered by government procrastination they vowed to continue their occupation and for the first time threatened to use their ultimate weapon — a refusal to sow.

This stand brought Walesa to Rzeszow and tested the government's resolve to end its obstructionism and grant the farmers their union. Within days of Walesa's entrance as mediator in the dispute the farmers won two important demands: increased state funds to private agriculture and the sale of unused state lands to independent farmers.

But they didn't get their union — and the farmers knew that without a strong organization their accords with the state would be worthless. To this end three farmers' groups, who had been struggling independently for the same objectives, held a congress in Poznan on March 9th and amalgamated into one national organization. Now they could answer the government's charge that they were localized groupings with no broad national consensus behind them. And furthermore, with a delegation of Solidarity observers present, they could point to the obvious worker-farmer alliance that had formed over the past several months of agitation. (A practical example of this alliance: the 16,500 workers of the Ursus Tractor Works volunteered to work Saturdays to build more tractors for the farmers.)

It was at this congress, held only two weeks after the Rzeszow "settlement" that the call for union status was raised again. And at Bydogoszcz 150 farmers sat-in at the local party headquarters of the fellow-travelling United Peasant Party to press their demands. Three days later a delegation of these farmers crossed town to meet with regional officials at their offices, but when the meeting abruptly ended before they could speak the farmers demanded to stay to draft a written statement. As they were completing it two hundred riot police stormed the building, forcibly evicting the twenty-five farmers and mercilessly beating them in the process. Three were so badly injured that they required hospitalization, one, a 68 year old, was near death.

A General Strike Call

As if a lightning bolt had struck, across Poland the response to the state's violence was swift and militant. The instant change in mood was all the more remarkable because the last few weeks had been the quietest in Poland since the holiday season. Though Solidarity had not officially declared a moratorium, Walesa was counselling moderation and in some instances being criticized for undermining local struggles. It must be said though that more than once the mere threat of a strike brought results.

This attack however cried for massive retaliation and Walesa had not so distanced himself from the rank and file to think otherwise. The next morning as Solidarity's National Consultive Committee (KKP) was rushing to Bydgoszcz for an emergency session, a half-dozen cities had called 2 hour protest strikes.

The police attack occurred not only days after the initiation of the annual Warsaw Pact maneuvers in Poland, but also near a rail junction vital to the war games. One would have had to be an extreme partisan of chance to discount the likelihood of premeditation in this assault. Later it became clear that not only had the Bydgoszcz incident been planned by some high-ranking members of the party, but that those same hidebound elements pushed through the intital hard-line and abusive government statement on the attack. This statement accused Solidarity of creating an "atmosphere of mass neurosis" which was responsible for a "state of anarchy" in the land. Furthermore it warned members of the party not to participate in strike actions. This stipulation resulted in a tide of protest from local party organizations that, along with the rest of the population, saw the police brutality in Bydgoszcz as provocative. The first incident of organized violence since the August strikes, resembling the assaults that precipitated killings during previous periods of workers' struggles, was met with the most courageous, and at the same time, the most sober mass action the European continent, if not the world, had seen in generations.

All the previous confrontations, each building on the other in scope and resoluteness, seemed to culminate in this one. The whole society braced for a General Strike that historically would have presaged a revolutionary upheaval: the complete repudiation of the old order releasing an exhilirating surge of creative energy to shape a new society. And this certainly was in the air, but so too was the real fear that at any moment the Warsaw Pact maneuvers would move from the isolated fields to the factory gates.

An intense two-day meeting of the KKP in Bydgoszcz resolved to press the government for the immediate arrest and prosecution of those who inflicted the injuries, and more importantly the union demanded to know who had given the order to attack the farmers. This of course meant locating those in the party hierarchy (beyond the regional level) who would have had to give the go-ahead for this action. Furthermore the union (and the society as a whole) wanted firm guarantees that Solidarity and Rural Solidarity would be secure from all kinds of intimidation and to guarantee this, the list of demands recapitulated all the unresolved, outstanding disputes with the government, to wit: access to the official media besides a national union publication,a re-writing of the criminal code regarding dissidents and the annulment of the government decree setting a 50 percent limit on strike pay. And finally, Solidarity called for legalization of the farmers' union.

If these demands were not met by Friday, March 27, there would be a four hour warning strike throughout Poland to be followed by a full scale, open-end General Strike the next Tuesday.

A strike command was established to prepare headquarters in the Lenin Shipyards and to instruct all strike committees everywhere to move inside factories for protection from police attacks. This action would instantly create 1,000 fortresses in the country.

Kania convened an extraordinary plenary session of the C.C. for March 29, a day before the Parliament was scheduled to meet, and then had Rakowski begin the charade of negotiating with Walesa. Charade because the Politburo, already meeting around the clock, had still to devise a coherent response. Nothing of substance came out of the negotiations between Solidarity and the government before Friday and so the four-hour warning strike took place. It was one hundred percent successful and Western reporters in all parts of Poland commented on the odd calmness of this momentous event.

The C.C. meeting on Sunday saw local party officials openly criticize the leadership. From Szczecin a first secretary said: "We must know that Solidarity is in the first place the working-class itself." Another delegate, a worker in a computer factory in Wroclaw, stated that her local party organization decided to join the strike "even though we were aware we were violating party discipline. We read the events inBydgoszcz as a clear violation of constitutional freedoms and civic rights," she said. "We are part of the working-class. We'll never turn against that class. The guilt for the last strike is not carried by the determined workers who went on strike but those who brought them to such determination.''

Despite these criticisms the plenum of the C.C. refused to oust any hardliners. However, it did agree upon a ten-point reform program which Jaruzelski presented to the Sejm the following day. And while the Sejm was meeting to consider the program the government and the Solidarity negotiating team sat through seven hours of bargaining, from which Walesa emerged with an agreement he termed, rather anti-climactically, ''70% successful'' and called off the General Strike scheduled for Tuesday.

Walesa Criticized

When Walesa returned to Gdansk for the KKP's endorsement he was met with scathing criticisms of his actions and for the agreement itself. First, his undemocratic practices during the negotiations were attacked. For example, he was accused of sending the most militant members of the negotiating team back to Gdansk on the pretext of providing continuity on the national level in the event he were arrested in Warsaw. Next he dismissed the KKP's function of endorsement of any government accord by autocratically calling off the General Strike. After witnessing so many years of anti-democratic behavior in the party, the union members were not about to tolerate it in their own organization. Karol Modzclewski resigned as national press spokesman accusing Walesa of being a monarch.

The delegates from Rural Solidarity were especially outraged that they weren't consulted during the negotiations because it was obvious that their demands for punishment of those responsible for the attack in Bydgoszcz had been bargained away for government promises never to do it again. Union members also expressed their outrage that the points they wanted resolved for once and for all remained dependent upon vague promises of good intentions and still more government commissions.

The KKP, after two days of meeting, stated that while they accepted the agreement, they treated it as only a preliminary document and requested negotiations to hammer out specific commitments. In days however the atmosphere cleared slightly as two deputy governors from the Bydgoszcz area tendered their resignations and on April 3rd one-half million copies of Solidarity's weekly paper appeared unhampered by authorities (though it had to pass the Censor). A week later a nationally televised meeting took place between Solidarity and the government in which the union pressed for regular access to all media, the release of political prisoners and an independent union for the farmers. On the last point the Sejm commission studying the matter recommended legalization and on May 12 a court upheld this right and Rural Solidarity was granted union status after seven months of fighting.

As the tensions between the party and the workers and farmers eased those within the party became all the more visible. In response to increased local party pressure, for instance, the C.C meeting held to deal with the General Strike threat issued unprecedented guidelines for the selection of delegates to the extraordinary Party

Congress in July. The three thousand delegates the C.C. ordered would be elected in secret from an unlimited slate of contenders. A far cry from the established system of appointments that the rank and file simply rubber stamped. These reforms were exactly like those the Czech party adopted for their 1968 Congress that the Soviets cancelled by their invasion two weeks before.

THE INVASION THREAT

Newspaper readers in North America, unless they are fortunate to live in one of the few cities that maintains a respectable daily, read almost nothing else about Poland during these months of turmoil, except that a Russian invasion was imminent. The scare first hit the headlines just before Christmas and continued throughout the season, even though Poland experienced it quietest weeks then.

In January, as the Polish nation began to explode in strike activity, we again were visited with non-stop predictions from all sources that Russian troops would soon put the Poles back to work. A month later, after General Jaruzelski assumed the post of Prime Minister and the government began granting the demands of the strikers in the factories and schools, the barrage of invasion stories subsided only to return with a vengeance as the Warsaw Pact countries started their war games. It got to be that when Reagan, Haig or Weinberger weren't remarking on a possible Soviet attack, Poland wasn't in the news!

To complain about these comments isn't meant to discount the fact that the Russians were uttering threats because, damn it, they invoked more than once the Brezhnev Doctrine (the excuse for invading Czechoslovakia when it had come under the sway of so-called anti-socialist forces). The point of this criticism is that the constant repetition of invasion warnings didn't help the Poles but was a great disservice to them, and in this sense it played into the hands of the Russians. We must not forget that while we were reading these sensational headlines every morning, the Poles were hearing about them every evening as they tuned to Western radio broadcasts. And for them it was a matter of enduring a daily Sword of Damocles.

People have speculated on the reason for these on again, off again predictions. According to reports some Poles felt it was simply propaganda aimed not at the Russians, but at the Europeans who are reluctant to accept a continued arms race. Whatever the reasons for it however, it was more than foolish, it was brutal for the Poles.

As the summer approaches in Poland, food shortages continue to plague the population and rationing has been extended to cover many items besides meat. But for all the economic problems that beset the Poles there appears a renewed vigor to remake the society.

THE POLISH SITUATION: BACKGROUND AND PERSPECTIVES

—By George Kolankiewicz

(The following article by George Kolankiewicz was originally written for the Labour Party's European affairs subcommittee. It is published for the first time.)

The existing situation of 'dual power' in Poland is at best politically unstable. The independent trade unions cannot be integrated into the present system and major economic and political transformations must be on the agenda. Poland has entered unchartered waters and the course taken in practice to resolve the country's basic structural contradictions will outpace any theoretical understanding we can draw upon from the past.

BACKGROUND

Economic factors

After an extraordinarily rapid growth in real wages during the early seventies largely fostered by foreign credits, there has been a sharp drop in average real wages since 1976, with negative growth in 1978 and 1979. Inflation is almost certainly in double figures, having reached 8.7 per cent in 1978, although much of this is what economists call 'repressed inflation' and is much higher than the figures would indicate. Associated with this was a shortage of services and consumer goods, aggravated by an explosion in consumer aspirations which in turn was tied to the demographic structure of the population. The subsequent growth in the 'second' or 'parallel' economies, i.e. black market activity, intensified the criticism by those excluded from it such as the industrial manual workers, of corruption at higher levels. Finally the relationship between effort and reward was made more and more opaque both on the shop floor, where wages lost any connection with productivity and in the system of concealed privilege which pervaded more areas of life as the crisis deepened. Whereas real wage growth bought off the working class after 1970 there was no substitute for a genuine programme of reform once the coffers were empty.

Political factors

Whatever the Communist Party's intentions concerning **internal** Party reform and **external** relations with society after the shock of 1970/71, the actual changes were largely cosmetic (i.e. consultations, direct contact of Central Committee with key enterprises etc.). A policy of what can only be termed 'selective incorporation', where the Party sought to recruit key sections of the working class into its ranks, was used as a substitute for internal democracy. Again the opinions of the rank-and-file and lower levels of the Party were ignored by the centre and as the economic crisis loomed centralist order replaced even the few gestures that had been made in the direction of democracy.

The Party apparat, particularly at its intermediate levels, is staffed by what can kindly be termed 'careerists' who neither can nor wish to understand the **qualitatively** new working class which has emerged during the 1970s (no one had, nor in the given conditions could they have had, any real idea of the nature of the young working class which was the motor force of the Polish August). At best ideologically neutral, concerned largely with making sure they are backing the right leader, the middle-apparat of the Party sees current demands for 'democracy' and 'rotation of personnel' simply in terms of their reaching the power centre. During the 1970s the Party came to represent the ascendency of form, i.e. hierarchical institution of power with little content. To that extent the free trade union movement is the **most positive** event which could have happened to the Party and how the latter reacts to the present situation will determine whether it regains legitimacy both in the eyes of its members and of the wider society. Needless to say, the current anti-corruption campaign being waged is in part a feature of the internal struggle for power between competing groups within the elite and between the elite and the ascendent **local** apparat, but it is also a means of channelling the animosity and concern felt at the corruption of most senior figures in government in a *cause celebre* (eg. Tyranski and Minex). Apart from this it represents a reaction to the deep-seated system of privilege which the Gierek period had spawned.

Sociological factors

These are associated largely with the nature and make-up of the Polish working class. It required a cataclysmic event such as the Gdansk-inspired strikes to expose the sophistication, awareness, self-discipline and most importantly, self-assuredness of the Polish working class. The Party leadership had developed its relationship to the working class during the 50s and 60s, when the latter was less educated, less confident and less demanding. The number of young workers, with good educational credentials, (due paradoxically to blocked upward movement and failed 'co-optation') skilled, often Party members, who dominated the strike committees indicated not just the breadth of the generation gap (i.e. older workers tended to control the union structure) but the gulf between the official view of the working class which informed the decisions of the leadership and the reality.

THE FREE AND SELF-MANAGING TRADE UNIONS

Organized under the umbrella of 'Solidarity' into 17 territorial associations, in this form the new unions can only be **political**. The horizontal territorial link provides strength to such groups as teachers and academics who have little independent muscle. At the same time there are vertical, branch groupings which are engaged in the grass-roots conflict for membership, representation etc. with the 'transformed' official (but now 'independent' of the all-but defunct Central Council of Trade Unions) trade unions. The problem of legally institutionalizing the unions has not so much been resolved as postponed by a compromise until a future date. Whilst Party members are urged to Join the free unions the attitude of the latter to the Party is more problematic. The Party has attacked the exclusion of its own officials from holding office in the union, calling it discrimination. (Of course, under the old system of the nomenklatura controlled by the party, office in such organizations was the exclusive gift of Party officialdom.) This represents the tendency amongst unionists to by-pass or make irrelevant Party control within the trade union and is indicative of the deep-seated disenchantment felt by these activists towards the Party and towards socialist ideology, as the latter is presented in Poland.

The effect of the last twenty years has been the effective 'de-ideologizing' in this sense of the working class. Evidence of the latter is the symbolism of Church allegiance, which is not so much a sign of the positive mobilizing potential of the Church amongst the working class but more of the latter's **rejection** of the Party as it stands. It is impossible to underestimate the cynicism and suspicion with which the workers treat the manoeuvres of the Party, aimed at satisfying working class demands but which fall short of institutional changes—a repeat of the post-1970 rituals is not possible.

The membership of Solidarity, 6 million or so, represents the **core** of the occupationally active population outside of agriculture, the rest being the fragmented and auxiliary occupations as well as sections of the white-collar and clerical staffs.

CONCLUSION

Short of external intervention, this is only the beginning of a protracted struggle for which the Solidarity movement is prepared. Every point of the Gdansk agreement, the eventual parliamentary legislation concerning trade unions, will provide new foci for conflict between the apparat and State bureaucracy and the union movement. The significance of what will emerge for the future of the Soviet bloc countries is inestimable. However, the movement towards free trade unions and the aspirations which have been released will not disappear and any external policy must recognize the **permanence** of the legacy of the summer of 1980.

The first issue of the strike bulletin

ii THE STRIKE BULLETIN 'SOLIDARNOŚĆ'

One of the first things which striking workers run up against is the concentration of the press in the hands of forces hostile to their strike. And everywhere, too, the workers' response has been to use whatever technical means are available to counter the officials lies and inform both each other and the wider public of their real demands and the actual course of the strike. The Gdansk shipyard workers proved no exception to this rule. Beginning with primitive leaflets announcing their early demands, they progressed to a four-page strike bulletin Solidarność **which appeared every day between 23 August and the end of the action.**

The thirteen issues of Solidarność **filled with news of the strike negotiations and activity in the Gdansk-Gdynia-Sopot region, provide an invaluable historical record of the greatest strike movement in post-war Eastern Europe. They also contain one of the best chronologies of the strike to have been produced (See Nos.12, 13), interviews with strikers and other figures, replies to official journalists and government spokesmen, and a great deal of other material. In this respect, they are also a precursor of the much more polished weekly magazine which the independent union will now be publishing — a magazine which, in its break with the monopoly of information so central to the Stalinist political system, itself represents a by no means minor achievement of the strike.**

We reproduce below an almost complete translation of the set of bulletins, preceded by the two MKS statements issued before Solidarność **commenced publication. All pictures and captions, as well as the glossary on p** 171**, have been added by** Labour Focus. **Further editorial material is in italics. The historic Gdansk agreement between the Inter-factory Strike Committee and the government commission, points one and two of which appeared in** Solidarność **No.13, has been reprinted in full at the end of this section.**

STATEMENT NO.1

(Statement of the Interfactory Strike Committee (MKS), consisting of 308 representatives of 304 Gdansk region enterprises on strike, based in the Lenin Shipyard in Gdansk.

The first of our demands is of crucial importance. Without independent trade unions all the other demands can be ruled out in the future, as it has happened several times in the short history of the Polish People's Republic. The official trade unions have not only failed to defend our interests: moreover, they have been more hostile to the justified strike action than the party and state organs. Chairman of the CRZZ (Central Trade Union Council — the official trade unions) Jan Szydlak has delivered the strongest attack on the strikes; although he considers himself to be representing the workers, he in fact represents the institution which is responsible for the recent situation in Poland. In his latest statement at a meeting of the so-called activists of Gdansk province (with 14 representatives — a fraction of the existing factory councils) Mr. Szydlak did not deem it right to criticize the official trade unions. He described our strike as a result of hostile forces and terror. He threatened: 'We will not give up power nor will we share it' — he said, thereby informing the public opinion that he wants to represent us without our consent. Our mandate is for him of no consequence.

MKS and the workers on strike cannot be indifferent towards this official stand of the CRZZ. Our reaction is the decision of all the strikers within MKS to leave the party- and state-controlled trade unions. The decision was taken this morning at 10.20am.

Our strike enjoys the support and sympathy of all the country and of other countries in the world, because our 21 demands are deeply humanitarian. The strikers and society at large are well aware of this and it is a source of our strength. The workers are not fighting for a mere pittance for themselves but 'For justice for the whole nation'. We have to oppose the local authorities' attempts to disrupt the unity of our strike movement. We live up to the words: 'Man is born free'.

Only in unity can we find strength. On 20 August 1980 MKS also resolved the following:

Individual strike committees should not negotiate any of our common demands with state authorities.

Strike committees are responsible for order and safety in their enterprises and for readiness to resume work as soon as our demands are met and the MKS informs them about it. Negotiations with a government representation concerning the 21 demands of the strikers will be conducted by the MKS.

We are still calling on the government spokesman to undertake negotiations. Any delay of the talks means cutting off their own roots.

We were ready for talks already on Saturday 16 August. MKS is the only guarantor of the workers demands being met by the government of the Polish People's Republic.

Inter-factory Strike Committee (MKS) **20 August 1980**

STATEMENT NO.2

In connection with the increasing official propoganda of slander and provocation, the MKS wishes to state the following:

The workers are not surprised by the vile methods of psychological warfare carried out by the authorities aiming to provoke and mislead public opinion. Mendacious leaflets are being distributed which meet with condemnation by the whole nation. Everybody knows that the authorities are deliberately deferring negotiations. In this way they have once again revealed themselves to the people. The working people have never failed and will never fail. Today they prove it again with their political wisdom, discipline and a fervent desire for the good of the whole nation.

MKS — representing all enterprises — once again calls on the authorities to start talks concerning the demand submitted on 18 August 1980 by the MKS delegation to the Gdansk provincial governor, Jerzy Kolodziejski. Only honest and democratic dialogue can bring the strike action to an end. Only by listening to the voice of the working people and by meeting their demands can normal life be resumed in our country. Workers on strike do not destroy national unity and do not harm the Polish state. If the authorities want to find this out, let them come to the strikers and acquaint themselves with the resolution of the MKS which represents the workers. The truth is to be found here, not in the headquarters of the Provincial Town Council. Workers of the Gdansk shipyard — which is the headquarters of the MKS — as well as the MKS itself guarantee full safety of the government delegation here during the discussions.

Inter-factory Strike Committee (MKS) **21 August 1980**

(After 21 August, MKS statements were printed in Solidarnosc.)

Solidarity Strike Bulletin No.1 23 August 1980

LATEST NEWS

On 22 August 1980 a team of three members of the Inter-Factory Strike Committee submitted to the Deputy Premier yet another request for negotiations. The Deputy Premier received the delegation and acknowledged the request. It has been agreed that the Governor of Gdansk will conduct preliminary talks with the Inter-Factory Strike Committee on 23 August 1980.

On 23 August 1980 the Committee informed the authorities that they accepted the offer of the governor to initiate the talks. The Committee appointed a group of four members to represent them at the talks, which started at 2 p.m. in the shipyard. Taking part are: the Governor Jerzy Kolodziejski, on behalf of the authorities and Lech Badkowski (chairman), Bogdan Lis, Andrzej Gwiazda and Zdzislaw Kobylinski on behalf of the strikers. Lech Walesa (chairman of the Inter-Factory Strike Committee) and Klemens Gniech (Director of the Gdansk shipyard) attended as observers. It has been established that a governmental delegation will arrive to start talks with the Inter-Factory Strike Committee at 8 p.m.

STATEMENT OF THE INTER-FACTORY STRIKE COMMITTEE
23 AUGUST 1980

The whole country awaits genuine and accurate news from the strike-bound Baltic coast. But the news in the press, radio and television is both distorted and incomplete. The existence of the Inter-Factory Strike Committee in Gdansk, Szczecin and Elblag is ignored. Nothing has been said about the fact that the strike action is coordinated and directed by the democratically elected Inter-Factory Strike Committee. The plant committees empowered the Inter-Factory Strike Committee to represent all strikers in the negotiations with the authorities. The public have not been told that the governmental commissions — although they arrived — refused to talk with the Inter-Factory Strike Committee which is the only representative recognised by the body of strikers. The full solidarity of the strikers with the Inter-Factory Strike Committees, on which all the striking units are represented is being concealed from the public. All the attempts by the authorities to break the solidarity of the workers by trying to negotiate with unit committees or even with individual workshops have failed.

The list of strikers' demands submitted by the Inter-Factory Strike Committee to the authorities as early as 18 August 1980 and containing the crucial stipulation of the free trade unions, has been kept from the public. The attempts to negotiate with individual plants and to buy off small groups of workers with offers of large pay increases are presented in the media as negotiations likely to satisfy the whole workforce and to settle the strike. A false impression is being created that the workers in public services have not joined the strike. In fact, they joined us very early but continue to maintain essential services with full consent of the Inter-Factory Strike Committee in order to provide for the basic needs of the community and to safeguard public property. We are accused of anti-socialist tendencies, while in fact our demands are completely within the law and in no way in conflict either with the existing system or the government's political alliances. We point out that the lies about the situation and the intentions of the strikers destroy all remnants of confidence in the official press, radio and television, and they do not lessen public disquiet. We demand that all Poles be given full and accurate information about our demands, about everyday conditions on the Coast and about the whole situation.

Members of the Presidium, Inter-Factory Strike Committee

Lech Walesa - Gdansk shipyard Zremb (electrician), **Joanna Duda Gwiazda** - Ceto (shipbuilding engineer), **Bogdan Lis** - Elmor (labourer), **Anna Walentynowicz** - Gdansk-Lenin Shipyard (welder), **Florian Wisniewski** - Elektromontaz (electrician), **Lech Jedruszewski** - Paris Commune Shipyard (mechanic), **Stefan Izdebski** - Gdynia Port (docker), **Henryk Krzywonos WPK** (driver), **Tadeusz Stanny** - refinery (electrician), **Stefan Lewandowski** - Gdansk Port (crane driver), **Lech Sobieszak** - Siabkopol (metal worker), **Jozef Przybylski** - Dubimor (metal worker), **Zdzislaw Kobylinski PKS** (storeman), **Andrzej Kolodziej** - Paris Commune Shipyard (welder) and **Wojciech Gruszewski** - Gdansk College of Technology (doctor of Chemistry), **Lech Badkowski** (writer).

(The list is followed by quotations from the texts of ILO Conventions 87 and 98, both ratified by the Polish Government.)

WHAT TO DEMAND AND HOW TO CONDUCT STRIKES:

Strikes are the workers' most effective weapon. It is, however, essential to determine the demands to be submitted to the management before a decision is made to go on strike. Until recently, all demands tended to be over pay. Claims for wage increases have been and are likely to continue to be the most common reason for industrial action in view of the constant price rises. It is important to demand an increase in basic wages and not in the bonus, which can easily be withdrawn by the management in a month or two. It is better to ask for an increase of a definite amount, say 1000 zlotys and not for a percentage increase, which would benefit most those who already earn more. Claims should be made for cost of living allowances to be related to price changes and to be made an integral part of family allowances. When pay claims are put forward it is to the workers' advantage to discuss the over-complicated pay system as a whole. There are so many tables, groups, classifications and special allowances for this and that it is difficult to see what the rate of pay is. This makes it possible for the management to cheat on pay. The rates should be made uniform, simple and easily understood by all. The analysis of previous strikes shows that the working conditions, transport to work and housing have not been subject to negotiations. Despite the fact that the living conditions are often extremely difficult and that solutions to those problems are possible, people have got so used to their lot that they fail to demand improvements. The transport situation provides a good example: the time-tables of trains and buses are at odds with the works time-tables; both buses and trains run late. It is essential to demand improved social amenities and to negotiate definite dates for action on such matters as the badly organized in-factory transport, lack of air conditioning, lack of anti-noise and anti-vibration devices, absence of special clothing, lockers, the appalling sanitary arrangements and the failure to provide special meals to which some categories of workers are entitled. The strike committee should insist on seeing the accounts. Demands should also include a condition, to be acknowledged by the management in writing, that no one involved in the strike would be victimised.

The organizers should put demands in writing and make them known to all the workforce. If everyone is in agreement that they should be submitted to the management, every shop and section should proceed to choose a delegate. The elected representatives then confront the management with the demands and request answers. If the management delays or refuses to talk, further steps must be considered. The optimum solution is for the management to agree to the talks and the settlement demanded by the workers. In that case the need for a strike does not arise.

If the management refuses, the representatives form a strike committee and work stops. There are exceptions to this: stoppages which would involve very great losses, such as closing blast furnaces, or too much inconvenience to the community, such as closing power stations, must not occur. The strike goes on until demands are met. The workers report at their work places but refrain from working. During the strike, the committee is responsible for the workers' conduct and it must prevent hooliganism and drunkenness. In the end the management will have to talk. It is normal for the strikers to make some concessions and to modify their original claims: the strike is then settled. The terms of the settlement are agreed as well as the dates for their implementation. The terms are then presented to the workers. The authorities have in the past cheated so often that it is essential to exercise control over the implementation of the agreement. For that purpose the strike committee continues to function as a Workers' Commission. If the terms of the settlement are not observed by the management the Commission must make a protest and if that does not work, it may be necessary to threaten another strike.

Printed by the Free Press of the Gdansk Shipyard

Solidarity Strike Bulletin No.2 24 August 1980

MESSAGE FROM POPE JOHN PAUL II TO THE PRIMATE OF POLAND CARDINAL WYSZYNSKI

Beloved and Revered Cardinal,
I write to assure Your Eminence of my closeness to you during these difficult days. I am with my country and countrymen throughout your ordeal, with all my heart and in all my prayers.

The news concerning Poland occupies the main pages of newspapers, it is constantly seen on the television screen and heard on the radio. I pray that once again, the Episcopate with the Primate at its head and supported by the trust in Her who is the Defender of our country, may be able to aid the nation in its struggle for daily bread, social justice and a natural light to its own way of life and achievement.

A very profound need impelled me to send you these few lines. I am with you at the feet of Our Lady of Czestochowa with solicitude, prayers and a blessing.

With deepest reverence,
John Paul II

VISIT BY THE DELEGATION FROM THE SZCZECIN INTER-FACTORY STRIKE COMMITTEE (MKS)

We had a visit yesterday, 23 August, late in the evening. The delegates from the Szczecin MKS came to tell us that their committee established in Szczecin on Monday, 18 August now represents 134 plants. Negotiations with the governmental commission led by K. Barcikowski started on Thursday the 21st. The list of demands closely resembles our own. In contrast to Gdansk, the police and the security services refrained from interfering with the strikes. The telephones have not been cut off. Mr. Barcikowski appears, according to the Szczecin delegates, more flexible than the Vice Premier Jagielski and readier to concede workers' demands.

The visit of the Szczecin delegates is likely to initiate a regular exchange of views and we hope that it may lead to a long-term cooperation between our two centres.
The Editors

DEMANDS OF THE STRIKING WORKFORCES REPRESENTED ON THE INTER-FACTORY STRIKE COMMITTEE OF GDANSK SHIPYARD

The Committee represents also the workers in public service undertakings which continue working in order to provide for the essential needs of the community. The Committee hopes for negotiations leading to a satisfactory settlement of the strikers' demands. One of our preconditions is the reestablishment of the telephone service.

The following are the Committee Demands:

1. Acceptance of free trade unions independent of the Communist Party and of enterprises, in accordance with convention No.87 of the International Labour Organization concerning the right to form free trade unions, which was ratified by the Communist Government of Poland.

2. A guarantee of the right to strike and of the security of strikers and those aiding them.

3. Compliance with the constitutional guarantee of freedom of speech, the press and publication, including freedom for independent publishers, and the availability of the mass media to representatives of all faiths.

4. (a) A return of former rights to:

— People dismissed from work after the 1970 and 1976 strikes.

— Students expelled from school because of their views.

(b) The release of all political prisoners, among them Edmund Zadrozynski, Jan Kozlowski and Marek Kozlowski.

(c) A halt in repression of the individual because of personal conviction.

5. Availability to the mass media of information about the formation of the Interfactory Strike Committee and publication of its demands.

6. The undertaking of actions aimed at bringing the country out of its crisis situation by the following means:

(a) Making public complete information about the social-economic situation.

(b) Enabling all sectors and social classes to take part in discussion of the reform programme.

7. Compensation of all workers taking part in the strike for the period of the strike, with vacation pay from the Central Council of Trade Unions.

8. An increase in the base pay of each worker by 2,000 zlotys (?£30) a month as compensation for the recent rise in prices.

9. Guaranteed automatic increases in pay on the basis of increases in prices and the decline in real income.

10. A full supply of food products for the domestic market, with exports limited to surpluses.

11. The abolition of 'commercial' prices and of other sales for hard currency in special shops.

12. The selection of management personnel on the basis of qualifications, not party membership. Privileges of the secret police, regular police and party apparatus are to be eliminated by equalizing family subsidies, abolishing special stores, etc.

13. The introduction of food coupons for meat and meat products (during the period in which control of the market situation is regained).

14. Reduction in the age for retirement for women to 50 and for men to 55, or after 30 years' employment in Poland for women and 35 years for men, regardless of age.

15. Conformity of old-age pensions and annuities with what has actually been paid in.

16. Improvements in the working conditions of the health service to

insure full medical care for workers.

17. Assurances of a reasonable number of places in day-care centres and kindergartens for the children of working mothers.

18. Paid maternity leave for three years.

19. A decrease in the waiting period for apartments.

20. An increase in the commuter's allowance to 100 zlotys from 40, with a supplemental benefit on separation.

21. A day of rest on Saturday. Workers in the brigade system or round-the-clock jobs are to be compensated for the loss of free Saturdays with increased leave or other paid time off.

TALKS WITH THE GOVERNMENT COMMISSION

The Commission under the leadership of Vice Premier M. Jagielski arrived at the shipyard at 8 p.m. last night, 23 August, for talks with the Inter-factory Strike Committee. It is hoped that these will lead to agreement on the 21 points presented by strikers from 388 plants and therefore to a settlement. The meeting was chaired by Lech Walesa, who at the start, asked the Vice Premier to present the attitude of the government to the strikers' demands. As the whole meeting has been broadcast on the shipyard radio, we will give here only the salient points of talks. As the authorities have not complied with our precondition regarding the reestablishment of the telephone service, the meeting did not in practice proceed beyond the statement by the Vice Premier Jagielski. The strikers were disappointed as it was couched in very general terms and did not contain any definite offers.

Referring to the key demand for the establishment of trade unions independent of the party, Mr. Jagielski admitted that there was a need for a trade union capable of effectively defending the workers' interests. The present Act /of 1949/, fell short of these requirements, according to the Vice Premier and it needed modification. Our own experience, however, after December 1970 has shown that the agreement under which the Strike Committee was forced to join the existing trade union structure did not achieve a genuine representation of workers' interests. The proposal put forward by Mr. Jagielski, for new elections to the works councils, does not therefore represent a solution: it is no more than yet another sly attempt to avoid discussion on the establishment of free trade unions. The Vice Premier repeatedly refused to publish in the media the full text of our demands (no. 5 on our list). Demands for the 'guarantee of the right to strike' (no. 7 on our list) required, according to Mr. Jagielski, further thorough discussion but he assured us that there will be no victimisation of the strikers or their supporters. The Vice Premier appeared surprised by the news of harassment of some strike supporters and promised to investigate our allegations. We repeat that the Vice Premier promised us that neither the strikers nor anyone who supported us shall suffer for it.

It seems worthwhile to remind you that Mr. Jagielski expressed his 'sincere' belief in the existence in Poland of freedom of speech and publication as guaranteed in the Constitution. He remarked that 'censorship should be made to work more smoothly'. The Vice Premier dismissed demands for putting an end to repressive measures against independent publications, described by him as anti-socialist and socially harmful. Mr. Jagielski conceded that our economic demands were right in principle (except point no. 14 stipulating lowering the retirement age) but it was out of the question, in his opinion, to implement them in the present economic situation. This he illustrated with a great many figures to prove that such innovations would bring the country to ruin. Only partial changes could be considered at the moment but he omitted to specify what they were. To sum up, the statement by the leader of the governmental commission was vague, filled with platitudes, at times inept and devoid of any definite proposals. It is possible that it was meant to do no more than to establish contact with the Inter-factory Strike Committee before today's meeting of the Party Central Committee. We must hope that the government commission, having started the talks, will now consider seriously the matter of allowing free trade unions, crucial for the settlement of the strike.

The Editors

LETTER FROM THE SECRETARIAT OF THE PARTY CENTRAL COMMITTEE, 19 AUGUST 1980

We have obtained a copy of a letter sent out by the Secretariat to all Party members. It concerns the attitude of the Party to the present wave of strikes. We quote from it without comment. It displays a blinding obtuseness of approach:

'...the anti-socialist elements amongst the Gdansk Shipyard workers made political demands and hostile stipulations in order to seize control of the strike. Their demands threaten the essential security of the country. They put in danger our national survival, our common achievement and our unity built at such a high price and in such difficult conditions, at the cost of so many sacrifices. The most important of their demands are those concerning free trade unions, changes in the electoral law /there is no such demand on our list — Editorial Committee/, removal of the media controls and freeing of political prisoners.

'Those demands have one purpose only: to give the anti-socialist campaign directed against the vital interests of the working class and the state at least a jumping off point, if not complete freedom of action ... those political enemies demand the establishment of free trade unions not for the sake of a better representation of the workers' interests but in order to obtain a platform for activities aimed against our party and the people's democracy. The call for the alteration in the electoral law aims at the very core of our constitution which the concerned effort of the democratic, progressive and patriotic political elements representing the whole nation have built ... They demand the release of political prisoners but there are no political prisoners in this country .... this is accompanied by acts of terror and intimidation against anyone who is not with them, against anyone who dares to question their demands. The anti-socialist forces aim to introduce their own system in the factories under their control ... All of us must realise that our safety and our independence are not secured forever. They depend on national sense, unity and discretion, in our own effort and on the solidarity of our people with our government. The disturbances in Gdansk and Gdynia have already encouraged the West German revisionists, who openly admit that the recent events in Gdansk and in other towns on the Baltic coast are extremely welcome to them ... We must support the public services, the police and the security services who are in charge of law and order ... Our party is a party of struggle and of toil. This indeed is the time for toil but we have been also called to a battle. This battle we have to win...'

Printed by the Free Press of the Gdansk Shipyard

Solidarity Strike Bulletin No.3 25 August 1980

EDITORIAL STATEMENT

Early this morning leaflets signed by the district National Unity Front were distributed in the town. These leaflets accuse the MKS of refusing to enter into discussions with the Government Commission "despite being invited to do so".

The dishonesty of this action and of the charges made against the strikers can be judged from the fact that the leaflets were distributed only a few hours after the Government Commission left the shipyard. This commission came to the shipyard at the invitation of the MKS. The leaflet gives the lie to the statement of the Deputy Premier Jagielski who emphasised yesterday his willingness to enter into frank discussions. It has taken just a few hours for the words of the Deputy Premier to be revealed as completely empty.

25August 1980

LETTER OF AUGUST 22 FROM POZNAN INTELLECTUALS

To the Inter-factory Strike Committees of Gdansk and Szczecin and to all Polish workers on strike:

'We support your just demands. They are of importance to each and every one of us. We are full of admiration for your dignity with which you have conducted the struggle for your rights, which are also ours.

Your actions have demonstrated your capacity to undertake the economic, political and social rebuilding of the nation.'
(There follows a list of 34 signatures.)

THE APPEAL OF THE INTELLECTUALS

The present moment may prove to be critical for our country. Nobody, however, can claim that he was taken by surprise by recent events. There was no shortage of danger signs, heralding the coming of the economic and political crisis. These signs were, however, ignored — and the crisis came. It arrived as a result of years of ill-considered economic decisions, and the authorities' assumption that they were infallible. It was a result of broken promises, of all the attempts made to suppress the crisis, of disregard for civil rights. Once again it became clear that it is impossible to rule the Polish nation without listening to its voice. With determination and maturity, Polish workers are fighting for the right to a better and more dignified life. The place of all the progressive intelligentsia in this fight is on the side of the workers. This is the Polish tradition and this is the requirement of the moment.

Now, all depends on the choice of the way out of the present crisis. We appeal to the political leadership and to the striking workers to choose the path of negotiations, the path of compromise. Nobody should be allowed to gamble with the fate of the country and nobody should be allowed blindly to wreck our hopes for a better future. Nobody is allowed to resort to any acts of lawlessness or force, or to a challenge. We must not allow the tragedy of 10 years ago to repeat itself — we must prevent the spilling of blood.

The overriding requirement of the Polish national interest today is the immediate inauguration of negotiations between the official commission and the Integrated Strike Committees elected by workers in the factories and workplaces of the cities on the Baltic. We cannot afford even an hour's delay, as any delay can create irreversible, dangerous facts. In addition to the consideration of the material demands of the workers and to the guarantees of safety for all those who participate in the strikes, it is necessary to recognize the workers' right to elect their genuine representation. Freedom of trade union association without outside interference is a basic right of the workers, and it must be respected in any social system. In averting the most dangerous consequences of the present situation it is impossible to postpone the presentation to the public of full information on the state of the country. It is necessary to begin a truly nationwide discussion and to create conditions in which a common search for ways to improve the situation can begin.

All of us, the ruled and the rulers, must be guided by the good of Poland. In the present situation we must refrain from inflammatory remarks and from dividing society with ill-considered words and insulting judgments. There have been enough hate campaigns within our lifetime. We should learn how to observe each other's dignity. What is required in this difficult situation is moderation and imagination. To find a way out of our contemporary crisis requires the abandonment of rigid patterns, which lead us to believe that any demand concerning the necessary political reforms is contrary to the national interest and endangers the foundations of the system. In order to find a way out of the crisis the justified struggle of the public for its rights and for a better life also requires moderation. It is necessary to realize the difficult situation in which our country found itself. Only common sense and imagination can lead today to an understanding, which will be in the interest of our common motherland. History will not forgive anybody who attempts solutions others than those stemming from such an understanding. We appeal for the choice of such a path, we appeal for caution and for imagination in the hope that there is nothing more important for Poland now.

(There follows a list of 64 signatures.)

Warsaw **20 August 1980**

EVERYONE HAS THE RIGHT TO INFORMATION, AND EVERYONE NEEDS INFORMATION

(This article appeared in the Information Bulletin (KSS-KOR) no. 5 39. Some cuts which do not alter the meaning have been made to the original text).

These last weeks have confirmed an old truth: lack of information or misinformation has serious repercussions on the feelings and attitudes of society, and cannot therefore be considered as something separate from them. We do not live in a vacuum. The effects which economic difficulties and tensions have on the outlook and behaviour of workers depends on the adequacy and reliability of the information which they are given about the causes and the scale of these difficulties (...)

The absence of proper information on problems which concern us and on which our fate and that of those close to us depends leads to disquiet both for individual and for small social groups. When the problem is a problem of the whole of society, then this disquiet similarly grips the whole of society (...)

There is plenty to be disturbed about. Famine threatens the country. For four years a country which has not suffered from internal social and national disorders, and which has not suffered from any catastrophes other than those which are inevitable, given our climate, has been threatened by famine. For the last year we have been feeling its breath directly. Nobody can fail to be aware of this.

This famine takes various forms:

— the scarcity of meat and of meat products, as well as of dairy produce; the increasingly frequent lack of cereals, and of bread as well as of other basic food products;
— the non-availability of fertilisers, animal feed, energy and fuels;
— the lack of raw materials needed by factories;
— the inadequacies of the transport system;
— and finally the lack of energy, which is crippling our whole economic life...

Our poverty is reflected by the ever-growing queues outside empty shops, empty shelves in the stores, breakdowns, delays in public transport and finally, and most alarmingly, work stoppages which we don't want, and which leave us standing idly at our posts.(...)

Among the directives issued by the Eighth Congress we find the following: "It is necessary to point every part of the economy, every institution and every worker in the direction of increased efficiency." (...)

We would like to know, and furthermore we have the right to know what the purpose of all our efforts of the past 36 years has been. We have the right to know what has happened to the fruits of our labours, — which have not been small — that we should now find ourselves in this situation. I, and everyone else have the right to presume that the new "efforts" which we are being exhorted to make will be wasted just like the previous efforts were. Scepticism is fully justified in the circumstances (...)

For 30 years at least my generation, the one which is just retiring from the scene, and the generation which was born during the war have done nothing except work for the health of the economy. They have accepted to this end continual sacrifices, poverty and renewed efforts (...)

We are something of an anomaly on the European scene, subject as we have been to three decades of monumental errors and governmental reshuffles reminiscent of Latin America.

On what battlefront is it that we have suffered such great defeats? Who is attacking us so effectively that a quarter of our investments are wasted, and appear on the debit rather than the credit side of our national budget?

We are continually called upon to "take part in the discussion" on the improvement of work efficiency, on the accomplishment and over fulfilment of the plans and to carry out our duties towards our fatherland.

For many years I have been a journalist in the front line of those involved in the battle for information. I have been at my job despite being banned from working, and in the face of difficulties and interference of all kinds. I am thus well placed to know how much there has been that was worth discussing. However, when one says what needs saying there is no reply (...)

In his epoch-making speech of October 1956, Gomulka said: "The working class has a recourse to strikes only in desperate situations, when all the possibilities of discussion and negotiation have been exhausted. The strike weapon is the ultimate weapon of the working class." It is a shame the Gomulka forgot these words along with so many that he spoke (...)

The last 36 years have shown that the workers hesitate to take up this weapon even when they are fully justified in doing so. The wave of strikes which is now sweeping the country shows that the existing "order" can no longer be maintained, and that the workers want an order that conforms to their sense of justice, of sound economic sense and of reason. The people are demanding to know what exactly has happened to the dollars which we have borrowed, and which are now a burden to us all. This is more than a state or government debt, it is a debt incurred by the whole nation. Before it ran up debts like this, the government was duty bound to consult the nation, and it is to the nation that it will have to give account of how the money was used. (...)

In the present situation, the workers have nobody who they can talk to. The order which we desire will not come into being until the workers elect and give their confidence to authentic representatives. They must no longer be treated as enemies of the system, even if they have little sympathy left for the existing regime.

The atmosphere and the status of these discussions, so long as one is prepared to take part in them, may perhaps allow questions more basic than that of the price of pork.

Nobody wants these negotiations to take place in an atmosphere of tension. That might lead to a situation where the workers will discuss with the representatives of "authority" in buildings guarded by tanks and machine guns, and where workers will have to protect their buildings from attacks and provocations from the armed guards of these "authorities".

A situation could arise where those who are fighting for the right to happiness, dignity and to liberty are at one end of the machine gun, while at the other are the "defenders" of their own positions, fighting above all to prevent themselves from being held responsible for the situation in the country.

A nation which really wants to be taken seriously in world affairs cannot tackle its problems by means of an upheaval once every 10 years or so. Every nation finally has to grant, to achieve, sooner or later, even if it is at the price of immense sacrifices, those rights which will allow it to resolve its problems in peace and in a spirit of responsibility as befits the traditions of our people.

By Josef Kusmierek

COMPOSITION OF THE COMMISSION OF EXPERTS OF MKS GDANSK

Chairperson: Editor Tadiusz Mazowiecki
Members: Dr Bronislaw Geremek, Dr Jadwiga Staniszkis, Dr Tadiusz Kowalyk, Dr Waldemar Kuozynski, Editor Andrzej Wielowiejski, Dr Bogdan Cywinski.

The above named individuals represent the following specialities: law and political science; economics; sociology; and social sciences. The Commission is in continuous contact with other specialists throughout the country.

Solidarity Strike Bulletin No.4 25 August 1980

MONUMENT IN MEMORY OF THE SHIPYARD WORKERS WHO FELL IN 1970

The project to construct a monument in memory of those who died in 1970 was bòrn on the very first day of the occupation of the Lenin shipyard, that is on August 14 1980. The monument will be 30 m high and will be made up of four crosses with their arms touching, with anchors hanging from the crosses; the whole structure will form a circle. The figure four symbolises the first workers to fall in December 1970 in front of gate no. 2 of the shipyard. For 1000 years the cross has been a symbol of faith and martyrdom for the Polish nation, while the anchor symbolises hope. The flame which will burn at the base of the cross signifies peace. Let this monument be a reminder to all those who want to deprive us of our symbols!

FROM "EXPERIENCE AND THE FUTURE"
Warsaw 22 August 1980

This document, from which we are publishing several extracts, presents the point of view of people from differing professional backgrounds and political outlooks who set up, in November

1976, the group 'Experience and the Future' (DIP) under the auspices of the Scientific classes. The sole aim of the group is to develop a free discussion on questions which are vital for the future of our state and of our nation. Unfortunately the authorities have made it impossible to carry out any normal, sustained activity, and so the members of the "Experience and the Future" group have carried out a study of the most important problems. It has produced two documents, entitled **Reports on the state of the Republic and the ways to improve it**, and **What way out?** These documents, as also the one which we extract here, not only attempt an analysis of the economic and political situation in our country, but also put forward certain solutions, which "Experience and the Future" considers to be worthy of discussion.

During summer 1980, Poland has been in the grip of a massive wave of strikes. The workers' actions, and particularly those on the Baltic coast, have shown that the present policy cannot continue. It would be a mistake to reduce the present strikes to purely economic causes. They are acts of defiance towards the present system, and more, towards the basic principles governing the relations of power in our society. It would be a mistake to present every criticism of those in power as an attack on the principles of the regime, or to talk of a lack of maturity of the working class or of the malign influence of "anti-socialist forces". Strike action has become the working class's only means of expression, in the absence of authentic institutions through which public life can be conducted and which permit a real discussion to take place. The authorities alone are responsible for what has happened. They and only they are the ones who have provoked a crisis which should and could have been avoided. Even now they are trying to find various pretexts for avoiding a direct discussion with the authentic representatives of the working class (the MKS in Gdansk, for example). They are also attempting to spread misinformation with the result that social tension is further increased.

It is no longer possible to postpone essential reforms. According to the participants in the DIP, these reforms are:

a) To tell the nation the truth; radically to transform the way in which society is provided with information, and to enter into a dialogue with society at large;

b) To recognise the need for profound changes in the power relations between the authorities and society at large, especially in the following ways;

— relations with the working class; to give workers the right to set up real forms of professional representation; to recognise the right to strike;

— relations with the countryside; to ensure full legal equality for family-based agriculture within the existing economic structure;

to develop self-government amongst the peasantry;
— relations with believers; to remove all discrimination against believers;
— relations with non-Party members; to ensure full legal equality with Party members and guarantee participation to all in political, social and economic decision-making;
— relations with the intellectuals and the worlds of science and culture; to limit and clearly define the sphere of operation of the censorship;
— relations inside the Party; to introduce genuine democracy, remove all special privileges and make the inner life of the Party public;
c) To recognize the need to regularise and transform the functioning of the legal system in order to guarantee respect for legality, equality before the law, genuine independence of the judiciary and social control over the legal establishment;
d) To begin the work of reforming the system of popular representation and the electoral system; to announce reforms relating to the functioning of the state apparatus.
e) To put into operation projects for a thoroughgoing economic reform, allowing the greatest possible self-expression to broad layers of the population.

Both the inquiry conducted by the DIP and the obvious facts lead to the conclusion that the crisis which is gripping the country is above all a crisis of confidence (...)

If the situation in the country, and above all the economic situation, does not improve in the near future, conflicts and tensions will continue to occur. It is therefore particularly important to establish a dialogue with authorities and society on a firm basis. If this is not done it will be impossible to reach the necessary compromises, to find short term solutions or to plan for long-term ones.

The present situation demonstrates yet again that there can be no resolution of the crisis unless the government is prepared to take the measures necessary to establish a climate of confidence. The authorities must win and consolidate that confidence through providing the appropriate guarantees — for we have been deceived twice already — after October 1956 and December 1970. Without real gurantees no statement of intent will have the slightest credibility. Deeds, not words are required to convince people that the present situation will not be repeated.

Editorial Committee of the Group

'Experience and the Future'

18 Signatures

LETTER FROM THE SECRETARIAT OF THE GDANSK PROVINCIAL PARTY COMMITTEE TO THE CENTRAL COMMITTEE

Signed: Henry Bartkowski, 24 August 1980

There has been no fundamental change in the political and social situation. Disorganisation continues to prevail in social and political life. One question is being asked with increasing urgency: who will put an end to this impossible situation, and when? Why will those responsible not take the consequences? We are critical of the speech made by cde J. Szydlak at the meeting of the Provincial Trade Union Council, and above all of what he said about the object and subject of power. Distribution of petrol by the inter-enterprise committees has now spread throughout the province. It has become more and more difficult to repair agricultural machinery. The population is becoming increasingly convinced of the need for concrete discussions with the MKS. New strike committees are being formed in the enterprises; and more institutions are declaring their solidarity with the MKS demands. The MKS members have dissociated themselves from political demands. The number of enterprises where money is being collected for the strikers is growing. The striking workers consider that changes must take place in the Party and in the government. They also declare that they will make good the economic losses caused by the strike through working twice as hard for two or three months. The population is not impressed by arguments about the losses caused by the strike. Masses have been celebrated both yesterday and today in the main enterprises of Gdansk and Gdynia. Yesterday in sections W1, W2, W4 and W5 of 'North' shipyard, workers continued to return their union cards. Leaflets issued by the MKS are being distributed everywhere in the province. Discussions by Party aktivs, which are taking place at the government commission's initiative, have completely failed to make people return to work. Meetings of the party, the administrative apparatus and the executive have continued. Individual discussions have been taking place between militants of the youth organisation and trade unionists and workers from enterprises on strike. The leadership of the Provincial Party Committee has tried to gain access to the main enterprises of the tri-city but has met with only limited success. Yesterday we had talks with some strikers from the North yard and the Unimor repair-yard. However, we have not been able to get into the administration of the port of Gdansk or the Nanta yard or other enterprises, owing to the orders of the MKS (according to the members of the strike committee.)

The campaign of explanation, which party militants and the administration are waging, is becoming increasingly difficult. Sometimes, as happened to a director of the yacht yard, they have been expelled from the shipyard. According to information provided by the secretary of the enterprise committee at the Paris Commune Shipyard at Gdynia, a congress delegate, comrade Urbanek, has put personal proposals to the strike committee in the yard, which will be added to the protocol of the Eighth Party Congress.

Political work aimed at persuading the strikers to return to work is becoming increasingly difficult, because support among workers for the demands of the MKS is spreading. At Party meetings yesterday the question of improving Party work was brought up. It ought to reflect the nature of our life more boldly. It has been said that Party members are not properly informed. During Party meetings at Oswiat, militants raised the problem of the negative influence of the current situation on the ideological formation and personality of the younger generation. At the same time they made certain suggestions, notably relating to wages. They demanded that all the schools should go back on the same date. At Pruszcz Gdansk, some of the Party militants in the enterprises on strike have gone over to the side of the MKS and supported its demands.

In general, Party members consider that it is necessary to put an end as swiftly as possible to this complex and dangerous political situation. Yesterday evening there was a meeting between the government delegation and the MKS in the Lenin yard. Two thousand inhabitants of the tri-city listened to the negotiations outside the shipyard gate on loudspeakers. They reacted in various ways: shouting, whistling etc. After talks with the MKS, representatives of the strike committees announced that the government commission had not been prepared for the talks but that they could be continued. At the same time they broadcast a recording of the discussions on the regional radio stations, including those in the Paris Commune Yard in Starograd etc. The strikers considered the opening of the negotiations to be a success.

Solidarity Strike Bulletin No.5 26 August 1980

MKS PRESS RELEASE
25 August 1980, 3.55 p.m.

The first meeting with the government commission (Saturday, 23 August) ended with a decision to continue the talks. No date has yet been fixed. It is up to the government commission to take the initiative on this matter. I repeat that we have made it a precondition for resumption of the negotiations that phone links with the rest of the country, in particular with Warsaw and Szczecin, are re-established. We regret to say that despite the opening of negotiations and the important events of yesterday, that the commission has not replied, and that the telephone lines are still closed.

THE OUTCOME OF THE MOST RECENT CONTACTS WITH THE AUTHORITIES

Yesterday, 25 August, representatives of the MKS Bogdan Lis and L. Badkowski conducted negotiations by telephone with the mayor of Gdansk, J. Kolodziejski. At the end, J. Kolodziejski made known the position of the government commission concerning the re-establishment of telephone links. The mayor told us that the connection with Szczecin would be reopened at once, and that the one with Warsaw was in the process of being reopened. Fuller details on this would be provided by the head of the government commission when negotiations were reopened. The mayor stated that communications with the rest of the country would be re-established as the negotiations progressed.

The Presidium of MKS has decided to put the decision to re-open negotiations to the vote. All the delegations brought together by the MKS voted against, on the grounds that the proposals put by J. Kolodziejski do not meet the conditions laid down for the re-opening of negotiations. After the vote the MKS put out a special press release, which reads as follows:

Special Press Release, 25 August 1980, 7.30 p.m.:

This is to inform the delegates of the strike committees of the following: given that the conditions laid down for re-opening negotiations, that is, the re-establishment of telephone links with the rest of the country has not yet been met, the presidium of the MKS in conformity with the decision of the plenum of the MKS, has decided that the negotiations will not start today.

STOP PRESS

Last night, representatives of the presidium of the MKS, L. Badkowski and B. Lis, met the mayor of Gdansk J. Kolodziejski. The two parties agreed to resume negotiations even if communications with the rest of the country are not reopened — those with Warsaw and Szczecin have already been re-opened. An agreement was also reached on the matter of radio and television broadcasts. Tomorrow the press, radio and television throughout the entire country will publish the press releases on the progress of the negotiations at the shipyard in Gdansk. At the same time the local stations in the three towns will put out a 20-minute programme in whose production representatives of MKS will take part.

The Editors

STATEMENT OF THE CONFEDERATION FOR INDEPENDENT POLAND

During the last few weeks, Poland has been in a state of acute crisis, the clearest expression of which has been the strikes which have embraced the towns, ports and factories of the Baltic coast. This is an economic crisis which has revealed such profound defects in the system, such lack of confidence in the authorities that it has become transformed into a political crisis. The character of the strikes has also been transformed along the same lines. The first ones were a reaction to rises in meat prices and confined themselves to demands relating to pay and working conditions. Today the workers of the coast are demanding sovereignty for representatives elected by free elections not under Party control and freedom of expression. They are demanding civil rights and reforms in the administration. The law must be respected and the whole economic system be put in order. The ruling party is in the dock; being judged by the class from which it allegedly derives its pedigree and in whose name it pretends to govern.

What led to the economic crisis were errors committed over many years in the running of the national economy, which touched all aspects of life and all branches of production. Successive teams did not manage to put them right, even if they recognised them. Such errors are inherent in the system itself; it is a system from which the Party cannot depart for political reasons, for fear of losing total control over society. It has subordinated economic aims to this one political objective. For political reasons it supports a central planning system, privileges for socialized agriculture, unprofitable investments. For political reasons the government concludes useless deals which are not disclosed to the nation, for political reasons it wastes enormous sums on unproductive expenses like maintaining the enormous Party apparatus and security forces. The cost of the army is a special problem. This involves the plunder of the nation's property by the ruling state and party groups and the manipulation of investment funds according to the internal rivalries of different groups. Finally, for many years, instead of undertaking the basic reforms proposed by experts, scientific institutes and the people at large, they have been patching the holes by increasing prices and wages, thus simply increasing inflation. They sound the alarm and ask everyone for loans; in order to repay them they have to rob the home market of the most essential goods, exporting everything from wild berries to trained manpower.

The government's policy is contrary to the good of the country; for this reason, the workers of the most modern and most effficient concerns protest against it in the strongest terms. For them universal profligacy is evidently best. The people protest who have the most to say on this theme, namely shipyard workers, dockers, seamen.

But did the protests have to take the form of strikes, which brought new losses to the country and created so much suffering for the workers, their families and the whole people? What other form could they take, when the authorities disregarded all alarm signals and calls for reform, when they blocked all channels of information and consultation, gagged the press and destroyed the representative bodies. It was not the workers who chose confrontation; they were pushed into it. It was precisely the workers who gave the authorities, the whole country and the whole world a lesson in moderation, discipline and realism. Their demands were kept within the legal framework, that of the international convention on trade unions and the charter of human rights. It is the workers who are the agents of law and order in Poland today. And they have been met with accusations that they are threatening the system, being influenced in anarchist and antisocialist agitation; veiled threats with very familiar allusions to the menace from without are being used. As if nothing had changed in the country and in the world since June 1956. The government has said the same things as it did in 1970 and 1976. Each time it has been forced to take them back within a few days. Of course, the working class emerged triumphant from all these crises, but the Party had to render account for the errors committed in the past.

The present crisis has shown quite clearly that the authorities are not completely aware of the mood of society; the inefficiency of the higher Party apparatus has also been revealed. The striking shipyard workers and the workers of other plants who have come out in sympathy along the Baltic coast are not threatening socialism, nor national security. In the workplaces which they have occupied, workplaces which, according to the constitution of the Polish People's Republic belong to them, they have revived the principles and ideals of law which are far removed from the practice of the government. A great sense of national unity has been created, which transcends divisions and differences, a true sense of common ownership and responsibility for the country.

The workers and the whole of society know what the geopolitical realities are. This, of course, is a matter of protecting the country against intervention by the Soviet Union. But what would make Soviet intervention more likely for Polish workers? That they should demand a righting of the economy and the granting of genuine forms of representation? Or that the country should be plunged into chaos, opening up a chasm with the authorities on one side and the working masses and the whole of society on the other — a chasm that would become more and more explosive?

The strikers' aim is clear, immediate improvement of the standard of living and working conditions and the creation of real representative bodies for the workforce. Both of these are essential: only such representative bodies can guarantee that the concessions and gains made so far will be preserved and they are also essential for the proper functioning of the state. Such representative bodies can become partners for the authorities in discussions on productivity and pay, which would help save the country from chaos. In demanding such representative bodies, the strikers are thus providing a means of preventing Poland's economic collapse. In complying with the pay demands, the authorities have rejected the demands which they call political, and thus have stripped their concessions of value. We hope that maybe in the course of further negotiations, political intellect will rise above mulishness.

The course and extent of the strikes has shown that the workers, in a spontaneous unity of mood, work and demand, have overcome their lack of organization and the enormous difficulties of acting jointly and transmitting information. We trust that they will continue in resolution, solidarity and peace. We trust that, in the name of unity and in the face of attempts made by the Party to divide them, they will put forward only those demands which will find universal support.

By their actions, the strikers are expressing the thoughts, feelings and aspirations of the entire Polish nation. The authorities must realise for this reason that it is useless to attempt to use force. The strikers have the international trade union movement on their side, and the vast majority of world opinion. These are observing their self-restraint, the quiet, bloodless battle which, we trust, will be bloodless to the end, since we know that on it depend the fate not only of the Polish workers, not only of the whole of Poland, but of the whole of Europe.

The strike movement has presented the authorities with a fait accompli. The support of the whole of society can ensure that it will bear fruit in changes for the better in the life of our nation.

Confederation for Independent Poland
21 August, 1980

CHRONICLE OF REPRESSION

Calm reigns in the dockyards, in the other enterprises on strike and in the town. Even the distribution of leaflets in the streets causes little disturbance. Within a few seconds, thousands of people have torn the publications of the free presses of the city from our hands. This has not, however, prevented the police and the security services from ceaselessly harassing the delegates of the MKS and people who support the strikers.

On 22 August Marek Bogdanski, Tadeusz Siedlecki and Lech Strzalkowski (from the PTSL of Elblag) were arrested for 24 hours in Braniewo. Marek Bogdanski was beaten up in the police van, and all were interrogated.

On the same day Wieslaw Slominski (a student) and Andrzej Slominski (a doctor) were taken into custody at the police station in Swierczewski Street. The police tried to start a fight while arresting them. The two brothers were treated with extreme brutality, threatened, beaten up and maltreated in every way. Another man, Miroslaw Rybicki, was arrested for a period of 14 hours.

We are also aware of the sacking of an MKS delegate. This is the case of Halina Lewicka, who works in a store at Przejazdow; she was sacked on 22 August.

On 20 August, Mieczyslaw Sikora was taken into the naval hospital at Oliwa after being beaten up by police. The doctor detected a fracture to the ninth rib, and damage to the left of the lower abdomen.

The MKS receives many reports from people who have had publications and declarations of MKS printed by the independent coastal press taken from them by the police. In each case the police carried out an identity check. People who provide transport for our delegates or carry food for the strikers have been subjected to various forms of harassment. The police took away the driver's documents of Josef Arendt (of ZPKS), driver of ZUK GT 8474, and handed them over to the court. For what offence? Because Arendt took bread to the strikers at PKS Tczew. Andrzej Miczewski and another driver have also had to surrender their drivers' documents. They were giving lifts to delegates.

On 23 August 'persons unknown' slashed the tyres on a car of an MKS interpreter in Gdansk.

We ask everyone who falls victim to acts of repression or who know of such acts directed against strikers to inform the presidium of the MKS in the Gdansk shipyard.

Poems and songs are flooding in to the office of the strike bulletin 'Solidarity', witnesses to the spontaneous creativity of the workers. We hope to bring you some samples of this 'strike folklore' in each issue of 'Solidarity'.

We ask everyone who records their impressions, feelings and thoughts on the strike to bring them to the Presidium of the MKS and given them to the type-setter. We will publish as much as possible.

One day a woman goes to the doctor:
'Doctor, give me an examination!'
'You've come to the wrong place, I'm afraid,
I am just a vet.
I don't look after humans.'
'O, that's all right, doctor,
I feel just like an animal.

'When I get up in the morning
I dash through the house,
Panting like a dog or a cat,
I gallop to work like a horse,
I cling to the bus like a monkey,
Loaded up like a camel,
Defending my marriage like a lion,

I'm already asleep when
I get back from work in the evening, and
Then I hear my husband whispering
Above my head, "wake up, owl!".'

Perhaps you have some miracle cure
which will make me a human being.'

Solidarity Strike Bulletin No.6 27 August 1980

FROM THE CONFERENCE ROOM

Yesterday, Wednesday 26 August at 11am, the government commission headed by Mr Jagielski arrived at the Gdansk shipyard for a new meeting with the leadership of the inter-factory strike committee. Lech Walesa opened the debate by asking if Mr Jagielski would consent once again to outline the government position with respect to the strikers' demands, taking into consideration the fact that the Plenum of the Central Committee of the PUWP met on Sunday.

To begin with, Mr Jagielski didn't want to discuss the leaflet distributed on Sunday by the Provincial Committee of the National Unity Front, claiming to be ignorant of its existence and its contents.

He then gave an account of the government's position on the 21 demands. He missed out point 1 saying that he would come back to it. The most realistic demands seemed to him to be those dealing with working conditions and the workers' material conditions (points 8 to 20).

He promised that they would be satisfied as far as was possible and proposed that we should together fix a date when they should come into force, as well as the amounts of increase in wages and social benefits.

Lech Walesa then spoke to explain to the Deputy Premier that all these demands were secondary, although important, and that they had to tackle point 1, the one which deals with the trade union association, without which the others meant nothing.

At this moment the team of experts sent for by the government commission, without which Mr Jagielski rejected all discussion about the free trade unions, came into the room and the subject was at last broached.

The chairman of the government commission then spoke and summed up in a few words its position on point no 1 of the MKS's list drawn up on 23 August (see **Solidarity** No 2). Mr Jagielski limited himself to reiterating that he wished for reorganisation of the existing trade union association, by the election by secret vote of new officials in the enterprises which wanted it.

The members of the presidium of MKS, A. Gwiazda, B. Lis, F. Wisniewski, L. Sobieczek and Z. Kobylinski then spoke. A. Gwiazda tried, in his introduction, to outline the reasons for the wave of strikes throughout Poland, and in particular on the Baltic coast. He gave us the main reason the lack of influence of the mass of workers on the decisions taken by the government in the sphere of the organisation of social matters.

In the rest of his speech, A. Gwiazda showed that only the creation of free trade unions which were independent of the party could establish a real relationship between the workers and the government and make it possible to arrive at an agreement, the latter being the sole possible outcome of the economic crisis in which Poland finds itself at the moment.

A. Gwiazda also said that he couldn't imagine the operation of free trade unions without their own independent press, representative of the movement.

The other members of the presidium of MKS rounded off A. Gwiazda's spech, by citing article No 87 of the International Labour Organisation and specifying that it wasn't a question of dissolving the existing trade unions but of creating new ones independent of all external manipulation.

L. Sobieczek explained that there was no sense at all in discussing the official trade unions on account of their role in the strikes. It was necessary, according to him, to tackle the following subject immediately: in what measure should the inter-factory strike committee become the new independent trade union association demanded at the beginning of the letter presented by MKS to the government commission.

After the statement of the MKS position, and the call for the creation of new trade unions, the session ended.

When the meeting was resumed, Deputy Premier Jagielski began to speak and straight away asked the two parties, the MKS and the government commission, to proceed to a more detailed study of the problems concerning Point No.1.
The Editors

At about 4 o'clock, we received the following communique:

On 26 August at the Gdansk shipyard negotiations were continued between the government commission headed by Deputy Premier Jagielski and the presidium of the inter-factory strike commitee headed by L. Walesa. During the discussions the proposals concerning demand No 1 about the trade unions were presented. The group of experts attached to the government commission and the presidium of MKS stayed behind to discuss the working documents with the aim of clarifying points of view on demand No 1. The negotiations should continue today.
(Joint text of the government commission and the presidium of MKS 26 August 1980, 1530 hours).

WHO ARE WE TALKING TO?

Gentlemen! You are no longer talking to those who in December 1970 answered: 'We will help you' when you had asked: 'Will you help us?'

We are different now, above all because we are united, and therefore stronger.

We are different because in thirty years we have learnt that promises are illusions.

We are different because we have understood that when we hear the words financial reorganisation, this means exploitation.

Who are we talking to? The question is put as the title. The answer ought to be as clear as can be. With the government commission, with the Deputy Premier of Poland. Can one find anyone more competent? However in the conference room Mr Deputy Premier is always repeating the same phrase: 'I don't know, I don't deal with these matters, I haven't had the time to familiarise myself with them'.

It got to the point where to the question of a member of MKS: 'Has the Deputy Premier read today's **Trybuna Ludu**?' Jagielski replied '... I haven't had the time!' A frank answer — the meeting greeted it with a roar of laughter. Are these 'frank' answers the only ones the Deputy Premier is capable of giving?

The essential thing for the people represented here by MKS is the creation of free trade unions.

The dialogue about this appears, moreover, rather strange. When a representative of MKS cried: 'We want free trade unions!' Deputy Premier Jagielski replied 'I agree! We too are for the modernisation of the trade union movement'.

With obstinacy, MKS repeated: 'No patching up of the old stuff, no more sclerotic trade union bureaucracies!'

This sort of dialogue is reminiscent of that of the old man and woman in Mickiewicz's story 'Clipped or shaven?'

The grandmother: 'Clipped, I tell you!'

The grandfather: 'Shaven, shaven!' The old man goes wild, drowns the grandmother. The old woman, choking, sticks her hand out of the water, imitating a pair of scissors: 'Clipped'.

This short digression isn't naturally, intended to suggest that one of us is trying to drown the other. Let us all the same go back to our business.

This dialogue is in fact only a double monologue. The meeting appreciated this and howled with laughter.

What modernisation? What revival? Would you like to explain to me why Mr Deputy Premier doesn't hear what the presidium of MKS says? Why he doesn't hear the laughter, the healthy genuine laughter of people sincerely amused?

The atmosphere of this meeting is totally different from the old ones. Many things have changed certainly. People laugh, laugh more and more, more and more freely!

We could, however, take a poll to find out how the words of Mr Deputy Premier, who reiterates his sincerity and his truthfulness, were received. The answer was unanimous: 'The more the Deputy Premier insists on his sincerity, the more sincere our laughter becomes in the hall.'

'Does the man sincerely know nothing about the leaflets attacking the strikers distributed in the area of the tri-city?' 'Does the man sincerely know nothing about the arrests and rough handling given by the police and the security forces all over the country to people linked with the democratic opposition?'

So the question remains: 'What, then, does the Deputy Premier know?'

On Friday leaflets signed by the committee of the National Unity Front inundated the city. They read as follows:
'Strikers, you need fear no reprisals if you denounce the elements which are incompatible with the law of the People's Republic of Poland'.

No-one today would be surprised to find in the road another leaflet worded thus: 'Members of the government, you need fear no reprisals if you denounce the elements which are incompatible with the wishes and the interests of the Polish workers!'

The Editors

EXPRESSION OF SOLIDARITY BY THE FRENCH TRADE UNIONS

'I'm happy and moved to be addressing you, in the name of my union, in the name of the French workers. The CFDT is a trade union organisation grouping 1,000,000 French workers.

'The CFDT is totally independent of political parties, of the state and of every other institution. The French workers fight in the ranks of the CFDT to safeguard their independence whatever the political system may be. The French workers fight with the CFDT for better conditions and for the workers' control over the decisions taken about their working conditions.

'The CFDT fights for the freedom of expression for the workers, for freedom for trade unions, and for the right to strike. The struggle that you are conducting is wonderful and arouses the interest of the whole of France.

'The CFDT supports your struggle, and has launched an appeal to all the French trade unions and all workers for financial solidarity with your cause. Today we can give you 11,000 francs. Your struggle shows that all over the world, workers must fight for their rights. Nothing on earth can hold back workers fighting for the independence and the freedom of their trade unions.

'Long live the struggle of the Polish workers!'

TELEGRAM FROM THE ELECTRICIANS' UNION OF NEW ZEALAND

'The electricians' union of New Zealand sends you and all the workers the expression of its sincere support for your struggle and for the creation in Poland of a free and independent trade union association. Your struggle for justice for the community and for the economy meets with support from all lovers of freedom the whole world over.'

CONCERT IN THE GDANSK SHIPYARD

On 25 August in the Lenin Shipyard in Gdansk a concert was given in solidarity by musicians of Gdansk. Works of Chopin and Moniuszko were performed by Elwira Hodinarowa (piano), Elisabeta Hornung (singer), Jan Gdaniel (singer), Adolf Malinowski. More than a thousand people attended the concert.

WHAT IS THE STATE DOING?

The first conditions imposed by MKS for beginning negotiations with the authorities was the re-establishment of telephone links. Why is this first condition judged so important?

Right from the beginning of the strikes on the Baltic coast the authorities tried (and to a certain extent succeeded) to cut off the rest of Poland from the news coming from the Baltic.

The press wrote articles full of lies, the radio and TV were silent or 'gave disinformation'. It was only through the normal functioning of telephone lines that people could stay informed.

The strikers could thus inform their friends in other towns of the real situation on the Baltic coast. Reliable information could be written down and distributed without being subjected to censorship.

What did the state do? It cut the telephone lines and shut up the active oppositionists likely to spread information about the strikes.

Since 19 August 1980, 25 people have been arrested in Warsaw (these figures are certainly not complete), the members and sympathisers of KOR, the editors of the journals **Robotnik** and **Placowka**, intellectuals who had declared themselves in solidarity with the workers' demonstrations. Under the statute according to which the police can detain anyone they like for 48 hours without the authorisation of the State Prosecutor, Adam Michnik was transferred from one police station to another every 48 hours. In this way these people were imprisoned for a week in the police stations. Two of them, H. Wujec and J. Sreniowski, managed to escape during one of these transfers thanks to the help of passers-by.

In Warsaw the telephones at the homes of members of the

democratic opposition were cut off. It was the same in other parts of the country. We know that Zdzislaw Mnich from Bielsko Biala was seized and interrogated. This was because Mnich tried secretly to obtain news on the strike of the FSM at Bielsko Biala.

The same things happened to a miner from Nowa Ruda, Stefan Kowalczyk, to Waclaw Mojka of Tarnow, to Stefan Siekanowicz of Gorzow Wlkp, to Ludwik Werle at Wroclaw. The following people have been victimised: Pavel Witkowski (Krakow), Wojciech Sikor (Torun), Stanislaw Smigla and Konrad Torzynski. These people are militant members of the democratic opposition. By keeping its opponents behind prison bars, the state imagined that it could keep secret the news purged by the censorship on the situation on the Baltic coast. Will this enable it to succeed?

The Editors

Solidarity Strike Bulletin No.7 27 August 1980

PRESS COMMUNIQUÉ OF THE PRESIDIUM OF MKS

A working meeting attended by representatives of the government commission with the Provincial Governor of Gdansk Jerzy Kolodziejski at their head, and representatives of the presidium of the Inter-factory Strike Committee under the leadership of Andrzej Gwiazda was held on 28 August in the evening. Experts from both sides were present at the meeting.

The meeting was devoted to the discussion of the problems concerning the first of our demands. The negotiations will be continued. The results obtained by the working group will be on the agenda of the meeting between the government commission and the Inter-factory Strike Committee. This meeting, arranged for this evening at 2215 hours has been put off until tomorrow, 27 August, because of the departure of the Deputy Premier Mr Jagielski, who has to be present at a meeting of the Politburo in Warsaw (2200 hours).

THE COMPOSITION OF THE GOVERNMENT COMMISSION DELEGATED TO NEGOTIATE WITH THE INTER-FACTORY STRIKE COMMITTEE

1) President: The Vice President of the Council of Ministers, Professor Mieczyslaw Jagielski.
2) First Secretary: Dr Tadeusz Fiszbach.
3) The Provincial Governor of Gdansk, Prof. Jerzy Kolodziejski.
4) The Minister for the Machine Tools and Agricultural Machinery Industry, Andrzej Jedynak.

5) The President of the Department of Industry and Construction attached to the PUWP Central Committee, Zbigniew Zielinski.
6) The Deputy Minister of the Land Administration and the Protection of the Environment, Michal Zubelowicz.
7) The Deputy Minister of the Machine Industry, Krzysztof Kuczynski.
8) The Deputy Minister of Foreign Trade and Maritime Economy, Tadeusz Zylkowski.
9) The Deputy Minister of Communications, Stanislaw Wylupek.
10) The Deputy Minister of Domestic Trade and Services, Bielski.
Experts: 1) Professor Jozef Pajestka, economist; 2) Professor Antoni Rajkiewicz, social sciences; and 3) Professor Jackiewicz, jurist.

A DECLARATION FROM POLISH JOURNALISTS

The presence of numerous journalists from the world press and television is incontestable proof of the interest taken in MKS and thus in the fate of the entire Polish population. Those who have been refused a professional visa come with a tourist visa to do their duty as journalists. It is the presence of 200 journalists and numerous television teams which has enabled the Western papers to carry the full story on their front pages for the last two weeks.

A team of Polish journalists is on the spot as well. These are the representatives of the following papers: **Polityka, Kultura, Literatura, Glos Wybrzeza, Kurier Polski, Prawo i Zycie, Kulisy, Panorama, Gazeta Robotnicza, Perspektywy, Czas, Sztandar Mlodych, Zycie Warszawy, Trybuna Ludu.** A number of them realising that the version of events given by the central and regional press and the television departs considerably from the truth, signed a declaration on 26 August 1980. In spite of the great prudence of its form and contents, this may presage a strike of Polish journalists. Here is the text of this declaration:

'We, Polish journalists present at Gdansk during the strike, declare that much of the news published so far, and especially the manner in which it has been commented upon, does not correspond with what is happening here. This state of things leads to disinformation. The cutting of telecommunications and the impossibility of publishing materials which would show the facts in their true light is profoundly distressing to us and totally prevents us from honestly fulfilling our professional duties.

'We consider that it cannot but favour the solution of the conflict and contribute towards social development in the future to give the population the complete story of the events.'

FROM THE PEASANTS TO THE WORKERS ON STRIKE

On 20 August 1980 the Self-Defence Committees of the peasants of all Poland and all the editors of independent peasant publications drafted together an **Appeal to the workers on strike.**

The members of the independent peasants' institutions describe to the workers the catastrophic situation of the Polish countryside. They claim that the state favours the state farms (PGR) and the agricultural co-operatives to the detriment of the private farms. They describe the difficulties they have in obtaining food for their animals and other means of production. They complain about the costs of production which grow continuously, the abuses of the authorities and the bureaucracy who oppress the countryside, about the unjust pensions system and the persecution which the true peasant militants are subjected to.

'We have to talk about a disagreeable thing', we read in this appeal. 'For 35 years, the government and the party have been inciting the population to hatred of the peasants. No account is taken of our labour and our role as food providers. "Yokels", "tramps", "clods", are some of the epithets which we hear from the townspeople. We are received with disdain in the offices, we are detested when we come to queue in the shops of the town, although at home we've only got bread, salt, sugar and gruel. The townspeople want to get us whenever we buy anything. They let stories circulate about our incomes and our wealth, but you only have to visit any village, go into any house, to understand that these are only myths. The state tries to divide us and to provoke quarrels between us, we must do all we can to unite.

All we have written here constitutes our minimum programme for introducing changes into the countryside. After the stabilisation of the national economy it will be necessary to undertake an agrarian reform. We do not want a redistribution of land, but a new legal code, new autonomous institutions and a genuine co-operative system. The peasant should be free to decide everything relating to the land, except for questions concerning defence. If not, we will always be threatened by a return to famine. If changes are not made in the spirit of our proposals, fewer and fewer young people will remain in agriculture and there will be therefore less and less production. Soon the state and the party will have achieved their strategic aim, they will have destroyed the family farms.

The whole nation should be concerned about saving the family farm. You in the towns, the factories, you lack a proper trade union, your rights are not respected, but we in the country, we are treated as slaves. The head of the commune and the secretary of the PUWP have an unlimited power over us. At any moment they can take our land away from us, expropriate us, transfer our children to a distant school, forbid us to finish building a house, conscript our sons into the army in order to send them to work on a state farm. The head of the commune, not we, decides what we should grow, when we must harvest, without worrying about our profit. Often he sends us state machines to gather our harvest when it isn't yet ripe. In some regions our lands are being taken away and we are being given new ones. We are dependent on the whims of the head of the commune even when we buy a sack of cement, a three-foot plank or other materials. To obtain any of these things we have to write out a request, take it to the head of the commune, buy tax stamps. we lose a third of the time for production carrying out these formalities, waiting in corridors. In practice there is no way of controlling the head, no way of appealing against his decision. He may be capable of ruining the commune in a year but we can't complain.

As peasants, we express our entire solidarity with you, workers, and support your demands.

We will repeat, to conclude, that there will be no meat and no food on Polish tables if they continue to destroy Polish agriculture. It should be the concern of all Poles to save the family farm.'

The **Appeal to the striking workers is signed by:**
The Self-Defence Committee of the peasants from the Grojec region.
The Self-Defence Committee of the Lublin region.
The Self-Defence Committee of the Rzeszow region.
The Committee of the Independent Farmers' Union.
The editorial boards of the information bulletins of Zbrosza Duża, of **Placowka**, of the **Independent Farmer**, of **Wies Rzeszowska.**

THE CASE OF EDMUND ZADROZYNSKI

The fourth MKS demand calls for the release of political prisoners. In this issue of Solidarity we outline the case of Edmund Zadrozynski. In future issues we will describe the cases of Jan and Mark Kozlowski.

Until his retirement, Edmund Zadrozynski worked for many years at the Pomorski Casting and Enamelling plant where he was an official representative dealing with all kinds of grievances. In addition to this he undertook social activities independent of the management. He organised petitions by Grudziadz residents about many local grievances, and he also worked with the KOR and as an editor of the publication **Robotnik**.

In July 1980 he was accused of:
1) for a period of nearly two years inciting his son Miroslaw to stealing, and of making financial gains from this;

2) of buying dollars along with the other accused Ludomir Borowski
3) of persuading Peter Rapacki, a worker at Polmozbyt in Grudziadz, to damage the bodywork on his car, and of bribing him to do so;
4) of extracting 2,000 zlotys from the Malanowski family in return for writing an appeal in connection with a housing application;
5) and also of aiding the 'framing' of Andrew Wirzbowski in a rape case.

Edmund Zadrozynski was arrested at the beginning of July 1979. The MO (police) made their charges only in September. Thus they spent two whole months simply searching for crimes of which they could convict him.

From the police point of view, Edmund Zadrozynski was an ideal person for setting up. One son was a known thief, and the other son had been accused of receiving, and had been convicted by a court. Nevertheless, Polish law codes state that after a certain period of time has elapsed, previous convictions cannot be used against the accused in a new case.

The first and most important accusation against Zadrozynski was based on the confessions of his son Miroslaw, which were subsequently withdrawn several times during the course of the trial. One day Miroslaw swore that not only did his father know nothing about his stealing, but that he had also many times urged him to find a job. He also testified that he was forced to go to court and accuse his father. The next day he was in tears and withdrew his previous testimony and once again accused his father. Miroslaw Zadrozynski tells a very unlikely tale about the situation which existed in the family home. This twenty-two year old states that his father used to shut him up in the house, that he did not allow him out to the cinema, and that every time permission was granted for a trip out, it depended on the payment of several hundred zlotys.

Miroslaw's brother, Andrzej, also gave evidence in this case. He particularly denied that his father had incited his brother to stealing. Andrzej admitted in his testimony that police officers conducting the inquiry had tried to force him into a testimony that would convict his father. They had first promised him a speedy release, and when this was unsuccessful they used physical force, tying him up with belts and tightening them greatly.

In the same way the MO extracted a statement from another witness incriminating Edmund Zadrozynski, namely from Zdislaw Wojanowski. During one day of the trial Wojanowski himself admitted this, but the next day after 'talks' with the arresting officers, he changed his testimony.

The changes in the statements of the witnesses, their accusations of brutality by the MO, exerting both a physical and mental pressure, are characteristic of the atmosphere in Grudziadz under which this trial took place. All the witnesses' testimonies were made in prison, all witnesses are therefore in the hands of the MC which doubtless helps their 'preparation'. The Regional Court in Grudziadz recognised that it was not qualified to examine the verbal evidence and referred it to the County Court in Torun. To this day, the judgment in the case has not been made available.

The accusations of stealing of car parts also rests partly on the testimony of Miroslaw Zadrozynski and of Zdislaw Wojanowski. And the worth of their evidence has already been indicated. The court recognised testimony of these two precious witnesses as authentic on the day that they gave evidence implicating Edmund Zadrozynski, and not on the day that they rejected such testimony. But that, of course, is the right of the court.

During the course of the court proceedings the owners of the stolen cars examined car parts found in the Zadrozynski garage. None of these parts were recognised as belonging to the witnesses.

In response to the next accusation — that of providing Borowski with 90,000 zlotys for the purchase of dollars, Zadrozynski not only denied this emphatically, he swears he does not know Borowski at all. And it is likely that if Zadrozynski had been at all acquainted with Borowski, he would not have trusted him with such a large sum, for Borowski was a known thief.

Equally unlikely is the accusation that Zadrozynski attempted to obtain a new car body from Polmozbyt. The owner of the car in question was Edmund Zadrozynski and it had been standing in the repair shop at Polmozbyt for some 1½ years. Successive dates were given for the collection of the car, but the car constantly turned out to be not working properly. Zadrozynski returned to the repair shop on the dates given to him, checked the continued malfunctioning of the car, and paid the mechanic for the work already done on it. He was charged with going to the yard with the aim of wrecking the car, and of trying to bribe the mechanic in order to obtain a new carbody.

Zadrozynski was found not guilty of the last two charges. The Regional Court considered the remaining charges and condemned him to three years in prison.

Solidarity Strike Bulletin No.8   28 August 1980

REPRESSION. ADDITIONAL INFORMATION

On 22 August, the MKS delegation who were going to see Deputy Premier Mr Jagielski was stopped by the forces of law and order. In spite of their explanations the members of the delegation had to present their identity papers, which had the effect of delaying the first meetings with the government commission.

THE PRIMATE OF POLAND CENSORED!

As a result of the numerous questions which have been asked about the speech which Cardinal Wyszynski made at Jasna Gora, the priest Jankowski told us that the media, on which the Church has no influence, have only transmitted the passages of the homily which were favourable to them, omitting the passages which were important for everyone.

In these conditions the speech has been disfigured and cannot be considered authentic.

THE JAN KOZLOWSKI AFFAIR

Jan Kozlowski is one of the three political prisoners whose fate has been taken up by **Solidarity.**

Jan Kozlowski is a peasant of 51 accused of having attacked an inhabitant of the same village, Marek Pyrkosz, aged 24, with a dangerous weapon.

The matter goes back to the evening of 7 October 1979. That evening, while Jan Kozlowski was at home, a stone was thrown from outside, breaking a window. Kozlowski and other inhabitants recognised the man running away as Marek Pyrkosz. The police were called and after having listened to Kozlowski and his witness Kolano, they went to see Pyrkosz: the latter accused Kozlowski of having attacked him, his mother acted as his witness. Three months later, Kozlowski and Kalano were accused of having attacked Pyrkosz. In spite of all the witnesses, who were favourable to the two accused, and unfavourable to Pyrkosz, who had the reputation of being a brawler, Kozlowski was sentenced to two years and Kolano to one and a half years in prison.

To make this affair clearer, one has to know that Kozlowski had already been questioned by the Security forces for his political activities. They had already attempted to put him in a psychiatric hospital and his elder children had been thrown out of university.

STATEMENT FROM THE EDITORS

Since they are refusing, on one pretext or another, to let us broach problems termed political, we wish to clarify some of the ideas behind our demands. This seems all the more necessary to us, since the position of the government commission in this respect, as well as the attitude of the state, seems incomprehensible to use.

We consider that in the present situation there is no problem which is strictly economic, even when it's a question of technical or immediate matters. Everything indeed which concerns the organisation and the development of the economy, leads inevitably to a changing of social relations. Each of us has only one life, limited in time, but in our enlightened, educated society, engaged in common matters, the consciousness of what social relations are is so great that lies and the omission of certain questions solve nothing. We therefore explain:

1. We know the world political situation, we know that we have duties linked to our membership of the socialist camp and the Warsaw Pact and that we have to stay loyal to them.

2. We believe that none of our allies has an interest in us having a badly organised economy or an ineffective and feeble social effort and system of labour. We think, on the contrary, that our allies will uphold our attempts to restore order to our economy and increase its effectiveness, which is our aim and one of the conditions of the improvement of our life.

3. We consider as a result that every allusion, more or less clear, to the anxiety of our allies and to the possible consequences of our action in the international sphere, constitute an offence to our allies and to our whole society. In our opinion such a way of posing problems may, whatever the intentions of those who make these allusions, serve the interest of a small group of evil-minded people.

4. The Polish worker of 1980 is a conscious, reasonable member of our society, whom one shouldn't try to threaten nor to calm down, for he can't be frightened and he doesn't create disorder. The calm, the moderation and the discipline of the inhabitants of the coast during the last few days are the best proof of this. As for the support shown for our principles in spite of the inconveniences supported patiently by the population, it is the proof of the justice of our principles and the forms chosen to express them.

5. Our demands are designed neither to put in question the foundations of the socialist regime in our country, nor its position in international relations, and we support no one who wants to exploit the present circumstances with this aim: on the contrary we would oppose them.

We do not demand culprits for the errors committed; but it is essential to take cognizance of these errors in order to eliminate them and avoid them in future. We will leave the punishment of the guilty to other tribunals. Our aim is to create the objective conditions which will make it possible to avoid these errors in future, errors committed equally because of bad policy by cadres.

6. We realise that all this necessitates long-term measures, efforts, as well as the changing of certain practices. We put our confidence in the socialist militants and the specialists who insist on the necessity of fundamental reforms in the system of planning and the way the economy is run. We know that it is necessary to transform the price system and the way prices are determined. This is certainly not easy, nor possible in the short term, but we must embark on the process of change by making our socio-economic view public, and by creating the conditions for the participation of all those who work and who have the right to receive the results of their activity, in the working out of the destiny of our country.

7. We know that this is impossible without a programme which includes our participation in decisions. The lack of such a programme and of a complete and generalised system of information has, once more, led to the systematic degeneration of the life of a very large section of our society — it has provoked economic problems which have been added to those which could not be avoided because they are of external origin.

It is for this reason that our essential demand is the creation of free trade unions, for it is the only chance of avoiding major errors in the future.

8. The social and wage-related demands do not come from the sole desire to have more money. The essential aim of these demands is to suppress the scandalous social injustices and to give immediate help to a large number of people, not only the workers.

The representatives of the state say that this doesn't solve the problems. We know it well. We are often asked the following question: where can we find not only the paper money, but the material goods we demand? It is not for us to reply to these questions, it is the specialist who should do it: but before we have any solutions, we have to have people with the courage to say to the government something it doesn't want to hear.

But since we are asked the question, we will reply: it is necessary, amongst other things, to eliminate wastage. It is in reality difficult to demand an effort from the workers without guaranteeing that it will not be wasted or exploited by others. We think that the rationalisation of our economy will make it possible to satisfy our demands and also to recuperate the losses due to the work stoppages, which were necessary to make our voices heard.

9. Unfortunately, certain losses due to bad administration notably the harm done to our natural environment, cannot be made good. In this sphere as well, we will not look for culprits, though this will be necessary. It is important first of all to create the conditions which will guarantee that these losses will not be repeated. This will be possible when the monopoly of power is no longer transformed by this power into a monopoly of intelligence, knowledge and rationality. One cannot get there without decentralising power, without creating the conditions which will permit the utilisation of the professional knowledge of scholars and the collective intelligence of the working class.

10. No-one denies that the aim of socialism is the transformation of social relations, but the results accomplished up to now in this sphere have been greatly reduced by the appearance of unjustly privileged groups, by the inequality of rights and obligations, by the gulf which exists between the extent of power and the limits placed on its utilisation.

Among other things we cannot accept the present state of human relations and the way in which superiors treat their subordinates. We cannot tolerate the attitude of certain employees nor even that of shop assistants tired out by the bad working conditions in badly stocked shops.

We cannot accept the scorn which those who are what they are solely thanks to the labour of the worker and the efforts of the whole of society often show towards the workers.

It is because of this and solely because of this that our essential demand is the creation of free trade unions, for we have to start with them. All the rest will be achieved through the efforts of all well-meaning people, through true knowledge and hard work. By guaranteeing our right to a dialogue, and the conditions for it we want the government to hear the authentic voice of the working class, and not just the echo of its own words. We are the true representatives of the coastal workers, and we think that the workers of the whole country share our views. We are ready to discuss all problems and to ensure all our responsibilities in undertaking joint actions. But we can do this only if we have the confidence of the workers, a confidence that the present trade unions have lost.
The Editors

COMMENTS ON POINT 16 OF THE DEMANDS

The shortage of beds in hospitals, the overcrowding in day-care centres, and the shortage of medicines are inevitably causing a deterioration in the health of the population and form a heavy burden for the workers. It is absolutely necessary to have a rapid improvement in the stocks of basic medicines which are in short supply in chemists and hospitals.

The Deputy Premier has mentioned heart disease and cancer as the major common illnesses in Poland. These are European problems: in fact, here, the most dangerous illness is, as in the nineteenth century, tuberculosis. But since 1976 there has been a staggering increase in the cases of tuberculosis, especially in the age category 23 to 35. The figures are published in professional, specialised publications but the censorship does not allow them to be mentioned in journals designed for the general public. Why isn't society informed? Who takes responsibility for this?

Besides tuberculosis, the complaint of which we have the second highest incidence in the world, there are stomach ulcers (this fact was revealed at the last gastro-enterological congress). The increase in these illnesses testifies to the living conditions of the workers: overcrowding, scandalously bad food, total lack of meat for the children. Beef is unobtainable, chickens are fed on hormones. This leads to the physical deterioration of our people.

The ratio of doctors to inhabitants is favourable in Poland. But why are so many doctors absorbed by administrative labours?

The number of specialist operations is very low; we are near the top of the list for infant mortality in Europe. You have to wait two or three weeks to have a tumour removed, instead of the two or three justifiable days.

I would like to touch again on the problem of the intermediary medical personnel. Neither the unions of health workers nor the Ministry of Health value this work properly and, as a result, the pay is very low. The nurses work very hard and have great responsibility: however, their wages are almost the lowest in Poland. The low level of pay largely explains the turnover in personnel. Of 60 nurses who received their diplomas here in 1973 only 15 have stayed in the job. If there isn't a radical improvement, the quality of care will deteriorate further.

We announce our solidarity with the demands of MKS and we ask for:

1) The raising of our pay to the level of that of other services, for example the secret police.
2) Three years of paid maternity leave.
3) The guarantee of 100% pay on retirement.
4) 100% pay when sick or on holiday.
5) The re-establishment of the bonus for difficult work, the increase of the industrial bonus.
6) The improvement of the provision of medicines and dressings; free medicines for health workers.

7) The reintroduction of the half-price rail fare, which the bureaucrats get.
8) Increased pay for night work (until now nurses have received 13 zlotys).
9) The reduction of the waiting time for housing — an increase in the number of housing units allocated.
10) An end to victimisation at work for one's personal convictions.

Alina Pienkowska
Delegate from the health service.

Solidarity Strike Bulletin No.9 29 August 1980

FROM THE CONFERENCE ROOM

On 28 August at 11 a.m., the meeting between the government commission presided over by Mr Jagielski and the presidium of the MKS headed by L. Walesa. The negotiations centred on points three and four of the list of demands. The discussion on the first two points was postponed for the moment.

The negotiations were opened by L. Badkowski, member of the presidium of MKS. Invoking the cyclical character of history and the repeated interference of censorship in our political, social, economic and cultural life since the war, L. Badkowski expressed the fear that agreement on Point No.3 might only be of a temporary nature. He explained that it was not a question of abolishing the censorship, for there are economic, political, military and other secrets the revelation of which might harm the vital interests of our country. It was only a question of legal guarantees which would regularise the activities of the censorship and allow a full and truthful flow of information and freedom of expression for men of different opinions. L. Badkowski emphasised that it was essential to pose the problem clearly and to grant independent publications a definitive decree.

M. Jagielski retorted that the position of the government commission coincided, in principle, with that of MKS. Only questions of detail were left to be resolved.

Point No. 4 was presented by A. Gwiazda, a member of the presidium of MKS. He summed up in a few words the trials of Edmund Zȧdrozynski, Jan Kozlowski, and Marek Kozlowski, pointing out their tendentious character and the violations of the law that accompanied them, as for example the preparation of faked documents to lead to conviction. Andrzej Gwiazda also spoke of the brutal victimisation of the strikers and people who helped them. The lack of social control over the organs of the police, of the procuracy and the courts assures them the most perfect impunity, and as a result, arouses fear and bitterness in society.

Other members of the Presidium of MKS spoke of the necessity of regularising the activities of the police and the Procuracy. This should allow an effective control of these institutions and assure, automatically, the true independence of the courts. Only a rapid agreement on this point could lessen the tensions between the state and society.

A. Gwiazda presented the head of the government commission with a list of people persecuted for their social activities, obliging the Deputy Premier to pronounce rapidly on concrete cases. The head of the government commission promised to do this; he also promised to explain the matter of the letter from the Polish Episcopate about the falsification of the sermon of the Primate of Poland in the media. The Deputy Premier emphasised at the same time, that the intentions which inspired the interventions of the members of the presidium of MKS on Point No.4 coincided, in principle, with those of the government commission, and that it was thus possible to begin negotiations in a working group composed of representatives of the government commission and of MKS, with the participation of experts. These negotiations would have the aim of clarifying and elaborating the agreements.

The discussions were postponed until 1800 hrs.

It is time, in our opinion, that the government commission gave proof of some sort of understanding of the strikers' demands at a moment when our country is on the threshold of a general strike. The avalanche unleashed by the workers of the coast can only be contained by a radical change in the attitude of the state towards the workers of People's Poland. The time has come when the leaders can no longer turn a deaf ear to what society says and demands. We hope that they have already understood this.

The Editors

LATE NEWS

Since the government commission only took a position on Points Nos. 3 and 4 at 1800 hours, the negotiations fixed for 1800 have been postponed.

AN MKS AT WROCLAW!

On 26 August Wroclaw founded its Inter-factory Strike Committee (MKS). So far 43 enterprises have joined the strike. The demands of the strikers are the same as at Gdansk. Attempts to get into contact with Gdansk have so far had no results. A delegation of eight people who left Wroclaw on 26 August were arrested at Bydgoszcz. On 27 August two other people left Wroclaw, but we are still without news of them. We know, however, that two people from Wroclaw have succeeded in reaching Szczecin.

BRITISH TRADE UNIONISTS EXPRESS THEIR SOLIDARITY

The Inter-factory Strike Committee of Gdansk has just received a letter from an organisation of British trade unionists. The name of this organisation is **The right to work campaign and National Rank and File Co-ordinating Committee.**

The letter expresses not only solidarity with the Polish strikers but also indicates the problems which the trade union movement in Great Britain faces today. It is perhaps premature to consider the difficulties of the trade union movement of our British friends as our own; it seems to us, however, that they are not only worth us thinking about, but we should also discuss them. Here is the text of the letter:

'Dear brothers and sisters,
We send you our fraternal greetings and congratulate you on the success of your strike.

Your determination will be a model for all the trade unionists of the world. Independent working class organisations are a precondition for the fight for higher wages and better working conditions and the rights for which we have fought for many years. We appreciate the true value of your struggle for we often face the same problems as you. In Great Britain trade union officials are elected freely, but we have already understood that true democracy isn't just about elections. In our country, we are now fighting:
— for the elected representatives to stick to the decisions taken by our conferences;
— for the right to recall any trade union official who doesn't satisfy our demands;
— for every strike to have the moral and financial support of the trade unions;
— for the wages of trade union officials to be no higher than the average wage of their members.

Please don't hesitate to let us know if there is anything that we can do for you, to put our solidarity into practice.

John Deason
National Secretary

COMMUNIQUE FROM THE CONFERENCE OF THE GENERAL COUNCIL OF THE POLISH EPISCOPATE

On the occasion of the feast day of the Virgin of Czestochowa, the General Council of the Polish Episcopate, meeting in extraordinary session and presided over by Cardinal Stefan Wyszynski, Primate of Poland, sat at the national sanctuary of Jasna Gora on 22 August.

1. The General Council of the Polish Episcopate feels profound anxiety over the present state of social, economic and political tensions in our country, for the good of the nation, the state and each citizen.

The tensions have several causes. They express the discontent which, for years, has gnawed at our country and which is the result of accumulated errors. These can only be corrected in an atmosphere of calm and internal peace. The general council of the Episcopate expresses its esteem, both for the workers on strike and their committees, and for the authorities, for having prevented disturbances of public order. This is a proof of civil and political maturity. This attitude allows us to hope that the two parties will find, in an honest dialogue between the strike committees and the delegates of the political and governmental authorities a solution to all the problems. It is in the interest of the whole nation.

A rapid solution of these problems is essential. In their dialogue, the two parties must be ready to find solutions acceptable to both sides. The Poles must know how to talk to each other and resolve their own problems themselves and put their own house in order.

The agreements, concluded and accompanied with guarantees, must put an end to the strikes, so that the national economy and social life can function normally. The two parties must respect their commitments, in accordance with the principle pacta sunt servanda.

2) The General Council of the Polish Episcopate, being at the service of the nation, directs everyone's attention to the behaviour and action preached by the Gospel, the principles of life and justice and the service of the truth. Calling people to order, peace and reason, it emphasises strongly and repeats to all that the respect of the inalienable rights of the nation is a condition of internal peace.

Among these rights there are:
— the right to God, to full civil liberties, to religious freedom and freedom of action for the church, to real, not merely formal, tolerance for the beliefs of others;
— the right to a decent existence for each family and to public

education according to one's beliefs;
— the right to the truth, resulting among other things from a truthful flow of information, and from an honest dialogue between the public authorities and society;
— the right to know the complete history of one's country and the whole of one's national culture, the right to know the truth and to express it freely, the right to freedom of opinion;
— the right to bread for all, according to their needs;
— the right to private ownership of land in agriculture. The application of this right to the creation of conditions favourable to the development of private farms will make them more efficient, reinforce family ties, tie men to their native soil: all this serves the needs of the state in Poland;
— the right to labour performed with dignity and in the freedom the worker deserves;
— the right to a just reward for one's labour;
— the right to meet, to elect independent representatives and autonomous committees. On this last question the Vatican Council says among other things: 'among the elementary rights of the human person there is the right of workers to meet freely in unions which genuinely represent them and which help to give the economic life of the country a suitable form, and therefore, the right of each worker to participate freely in the activities of these organisations without being exposed to persecution.'

Here are some rights which are worth emphasising:
3. The Polish people needs a true moral and social renewal, to recover its confidence in itself, in its future, in its own strength, to awaken the moral energy and the spirit of sacrifice necessary to make the immense effort which awaits us all. It has to re-establish confidence between society and the state, without delay, in order to construct, in a common effort, a better future for the country and to guarantee the interests of the nation and the state.

4. The General Council of the Episcopate orders, in the name of the Episcopal conference, that throughout Poland prayers should be offered for a happy, satisfactory solution to all the tensions and the problems. The time and the form of these prayers will be determined by the ordinary bishops.

POINT 13 OF THE LIST OF DEMANDS

Point 13 of the list of demands of MKS says: *'To introduce the principle of choosing personnel on the basis of their qualifications and not on their membership of the party.'* Let us look more closely at the problem raised by this point. We have received the circular dated 16.1.1977 signed by the director of the Shipyard at Gdansk, Klemens Gniech. This circular deals with 'the unification of the principles and means of taking decisions in personnel matters in the nomenklatura of the Committee of the enterprise and the party cell'. In other words, it explains the principles on which leading personnel are chosen, as they are now applied. A brief analysis of the circular will clarify the meaning of Point 13 of the list of demands.

The director of the shipyard, in this circular, is informing his representatives, the directors of the departments and the heads of sections, that the executive committees of the party should endorse appointments to the following posts: thirteen posts, including those of 'head of workshop, assistant head of workshop, head of team, head of the group of construction workers, works foreman, and construction engineer.' The procedure which leads to the endorsement of nominations includes 'consultations with the secretary of the basic Party organisation' and the 'candidacies to these posts as well as the complete documentation on the candidates should be presented to the Party meeting by the head of the sector concerned'.

The circular includes in addition this remark: 'the nominations to other posts (therefore to all posts: to the thirteen mentioned above and to the others) should have the endorsement of the executive committee of the Party in the enterprise'.

The procedure consists of consultations 'which the Deputy Director of the shipyard has with the secretary of the executive committee of the Party in the enterprise on the basis of proposals made beforehand to the executive committee of the Party.'

One can clearly see the dependence of the deputy director of the shipyard — entrusted with personnel matters — on the Party committee in the enterprise. The right of decision devolves upon the party apparatus, alone authorised to appoint whom it thinks good to leading posts. It is essential to make this procedure independent of the party apparatus in order to be able to improve the situation in the enterprise.

The circular also mentions trips abroad. Here is what the director of the shipyard says on this subject: 'Candidates proposed for a trip abroad to sign contracts there and discuss their technical methods, to study them there, to attend conferences and symposia there, and to consult scholars, to be entrusted there with the technical reception of ships or drawing up contracts, must be submitted to the endorsement of the Party secretary.'

The question inevitably arises: is the Party committee really competent in all these spheres? Or is it rather a matter of making the whole enterprise dependent on the Party? It seems to us that the Party, in its desire to control and to patronise the whole of production, forgets that authority is a matter of trust, of honesty and of authentic links with society. The party has lost this authority and it will have trouble recovering it.

The Editors

COMMUNIQUE OF THE PRESIDIUM OF MKS THURSDAY 28 AUGUST (A.M.)

On Wednesday afternoon, we continued the negotiations of the working group formed by the government commission and the presidium of MKS with the participation of experts from both parties. The negotiations dealt with the first point of the workers' demands, the creation and the future activities of the new independent, self-governing trade unions. It was a matter mainly:
— of transforming the present strike committee into the founding committees of trade unions, and of the MKS into a inter-factory founding committee of the trade unions;
— of creating a legal basis for the existence and activities of the new unions, and especially of the need to change the law on trade unions and for representatives of the new trade unions to participate in drawing up this new law;
— of the way the new trade unions will work, of their right of control and their participation in decisions in enterprises and in the whole country;
— of the position of the trade union that we are creating in the international trade union movement;
— of the attitude which the new trade unions will adopt to the present system in Poland.

The negotiations will continue when the presidium of MKS will have presented our proposals on these matters. These proposals have been being worked out since yesterday evening.

REPRESSION. ADDITIONAL INFORMATION

In No 8 of Solidarity, we made an error. Maciej Buczkiewicz, cited among those persecuted, is in reality called Maciej Budtkiewicz. Our apologies!

Between 17 and 22 August, Wieslaw Slominski, Miroslaw Rybicki and Michal Wojtkiewicz became victims of repression, the latter brutally beaten up by the police at the police station of Starograde Gdanski.

POINT NO. 4. ANNEX: THE MAREK KOZLOWSKI AFFAIR
Born in 1952, Marek Kozlowski learned the trade of locksmith. The first time he came before a court was in 1976 at the age of seventeen, when he was found in a coal yard with a few friends of his. Then he was sentenced to a year and a half in prison.

Shortly after he left prison, police sergeant Terpilowski suggested that he collaborate in a discreet way with the police. Kozlowski refused, and he has not since changed his mind despite numerous cases of intimidation. As a result, sergeant Terpilowski threatened him with death.

On 12 May 1972 Kozlowski was charged with an offence and taken into custody, only to be acquitted by the court some time afterwards. Then he was accused of assaulting someone, but the prosecutor subsequently altered the charge to one of threatening that person.

At the hearing, however, it became clear that there was no evidence, and that the supposed victim, Henryk S., was a drunkard and an adventurer who had been charged on several occasions with fighting in a state of drunkenness.

The regional court acquitted Marek Kozlowski, but prosecutor Krzywoszynski challenged the verdict and had him rearrested on the same charge (which is illegal).

After the case had several times been transferred from one court to another, the provincial court finally sentenced Kozlowski to seven months in prison — the exact duration of his various periods in custody.

Shortly afterwards, Kozlowski was again arrested and charged with two offences connected with the theft of pullovers and razor-blades. On both charges, the investigation was conducted by prosecutor Krzywoszynski and sergeant Terpilowski. At the hearing, it transpired that the pullover (the principal *corpus delicti*) had been stolen by someone else at a different place. The regional court sentenced Kozlowski to five years in prison, and he served his sentence in full.

On his release, Kozlowski began to work as an ambulance-driver and got in touch with the Social Self-Defence Committee — KOR, giving them proof of the crimes committed by two policemen in Slupsk. Basing itself on these documents among others, the court sent the two policemen to prison for a serious assault on Tomasz Kosciewicz. Mr Kozlowski was subsequently dismissed from his job as an ambulance-driver.

On 13 March 1980, policemen Wisniewski and Drewniak, who were questioning Mr Kozlowski in a police station, announced to him that he was going to be 'assaulted by some strangers'. And that is what happened the next day: some strangers beat and robbed him. On 7 April, he was arrested by policemen who beat him up in a car; and forty-eight hours later he was tried at a summary court on the charge of provoking a scandal in the 'Staromiejska' café. The police prosecutor called for a sentence of three months, but the jury eventually decided upon a 2,000 zlotys fine.

On 26 April, Mr Kozlowski was again arrested and charged with making threats (art. 166), interfering with policemen in the course of their duty (art. 235) and being disrespectful towards them (art. 236). Article 59 was also invoked to point to the 'hooligan-like' character of the offences. The alleged victim of the threat and the witness are one and the same person; and it was this person's statement which was the court's ground for sentencing Mr Kozlowski to five years in prison. The other charges refer to the same events (the café 'Staromiejska' scandal for which Mr Kozlowski had already been fined by a summary court, which did not consider the offence serious enough to warrant a custodial sentence). This time the court sentenced Mr Kozlowski to nineteen months in prison.
The Editors

AN "ABRIDGED" DISCUSSION WITH MR WOJNA, JOURNALIST[1]

Congratulations, Mr Wojna! Even without really understanding with whom you are discussing or what is at issue, you deserve our congratulations! So much demagogy in just one text! That's a real feat!

According to Wojna (**Trybuna Ludu**, 27 August), "a very broad range of problems can be discussed", even though "the actual questions have too often been set up in advance" and "the function of discussion in our society has been too reduced". But now, after the fourth plenum of the Central Committee, "we should start a discussion on various matters and sometimes (!?) on demands". Mr Wojna's attitude to the 21 demands of MKS is given very briefly and quickly: the points are just! And Wojna has even found a way of realising them: discussion, more and ever more discussion (quite different, of course, from discussion before the fourth plenum — no stage-managing, no cutting short!)

Here is a question, then. Does Mr Wojna want to satisfy all the workers' demands through discussion? Well, no! According to Wojna, the Party can find a number of political methods. For example, the satisfaction of the demand for free trade unions consists in its non-fulfilment. Yes! it is a demand which cannot be realised: it is **unrealistic**! What is realistic, then? What can the workers do? Well, "they can decide on the final version of the new decree on the trade unions, and even (!?) on the name they should be given". We are so glad, Mr Wojna! That really is a tremendous conquest for the working masses (now on strike). After long, hard years of mutual incomprehension and mistrust, the journalist Wojna has solved with one stroke of his pen the whole host of accumulated problems. The workers can invent a new name for their union. Simple when it's put like that ... but only a man on the scale of Mr Wojna could have found the answer.

But hark, Mr Wojna still has a lot to say! There are problems that cannot be discussed. "This framework is determined by Polish state interests and by the whole context — above all, the overall system and the alliances to which we belong." Mr Wojna! Who among us, in which demand, has attacked the system and alliances with our neighbours? What do Polish state interests have to do with the workers' 21 demands? Often in the press there is a method of discussion which consists in providing the enemy with opinions he has never expressed. The next step is to severely criticise what he has not said, and to pass over the problems actually raised by the person in question. Such a method is quite apparent in the August papers. It is also part of Mr Wojna's arsenal of subtle methods.

What else does Mr Wojna talk about in his article? About the anti-socialist forces, of course, like every "honest" journalist in Poland. It is already a tradition (and traditions are much loved in Poland) that whenever there is a social upheaval, official propaganda has recourse to these forces. (It is hard to imagine what it would turn to if those forces were absent). But the forces are there, and "they are joining themselves to working-class protests with the aim of turning its discontent towards goals which are alien to People's Poland".

Let's try to think for a moment about this last remark, so threadbare and banal. Is it possible that a tiny group of people (on the fringes of society!) could manipulate hundreds of thousands of workers while the Party, with its three million members, with the media at its disposal, can have no influence on these masses? Would that not mean that the Party, preoccupied with its struggle against anti-socialist forces, had without even noticing found itself on the fringes of society? We would search in vain in Mr Wojna's article for any explanation of what is hiding behind the anti-socialist forces, whom they represent, and so on. There Wojna has nothing to say.

To conclude, we would like to ask Mr Wojna two questions:

1) Why do you waste so much time and paper trying to deny the workers' movement all authenticity, instead of giving it serious thought?

2) Why do you force us to hold abridged discussions?

And lastly, a proposal from us for a 22nd point to be added to the MKS demands. No more Wojnas, ever again, no more wars![2]

NOTES:
1. R. Wojna is an official journalist who specialises in West Germany. He vigorously represented Poland at the last festival of the PCF, **L'Humanite.**
2. The word *wojna* means 'war' in Polish.

NO COMMENT

The following text was sent yesterday, 28 August, to the Party authorities of Gdansk-Gdynia-Sopot. It sets forth the Party position on the demand for independent trade unions. We are publishing it with a few cuts that do nothing to change its stylistic awkwardness or its general meaning. We thought that any commentary would be superfluous.
The Editors

If it were fulfilled, the demand for the creation of "free trade unions" which has just reached us would have the following negative consequences:

1) It would lead to a split in the trade-union movement: at least two central bodies, representing different fractions of the working class, would come into play. It would boost specific craft ambitions; it would assist fractional activity by craft-based groups, thereby weakening the trade-union movement.

2) In the current, extremely difficult economic situation, a split in the union movement, with the resulting divisions and struggles between various craft interests, woudl paralyse the activity of the administrative bodies of the economy, and would prevent a solution to the current crisis.

3) While it does away with class antagonisms, socialism also eliminates the socio-economic basis for opposition. In this situation, the existence of a socio-political structure independent of the ruling Party and the state power, would be a bridgehead for anti-communist western forces in our country.

4) The goals, as well as the field and methods of action, of the so-called "free trade unions" have been worked out by the anti-

socialist centres, which have profited from the fact that Poland ratified Convention No. 87 of the ILO but does not agree to the creation of free trade unions. The changes which we now propose for our trade unions are in conformity with this convention.

Profiting from the very tense situation in our country, the anti-communist centres have given the idea of independent trade unions to a number of strike committees. In several strike committees, the action has been led by individuals who have been known for years for their anti-socialist tendencies. These individuals are closely linked to the anti-communist centres in the West; they are directed and funded by these centres which are the main forces that want free trade unions.

Such unions would have the practical function of an opposition party — one inspired by the system of anti-communist forces spread wide in the contemporary world. They would give birth to a situation of dual power. Their activity would be contrary to our most urgent needs, and would also hit at our state interests, our alliances, and the related system of forces in Europe and the world.

5) Only a strong trade union capable of working with the government, only a union grouping together all employees and standing as a partner of the government can really guarantee the workers' interests. If fulfilled, the demand for free trade unions would rule out the possibility of such a representation of the world of labour.

Lastly, it is necessary to explain one more thing: in the West, free trade unions are a component part of the political and economic system of these countries, and where they have a reason for existence. In a socialist country, they would function in a quite different way: they would be a destructive element vis-à-vis the political system of the country. In the West, if a trade-union organisation demands something, it generally addresses itself to the employer, whether a private owner or the management of a company, and not to the state or against the state.

In the capitalist countries, unreal demands and obstinacy on the part of the workers lead or may lead to the bankruptcy and disappearance of a private firm. And so unrealistic demands are not presented, since they would involve the risk of losing one's job. In socialism, demands are directly addressed to the state, which divides up the national income at the level of society as a whole. Thus, demands which go too far in one enterprise are directly aimed against the others. This is absolutely contrary to our view of social justice, and so complete freedom of trade-union action cannot be permitted. This is why the anti-socialist forces are after free trade unions in our country. They want to bankrupt first of all its economy; and then, freed from all bureaucracy, all formalism and all demagogy on the part of trade unions which collaborate with the state rather than struggle aainst it, which are led by one political party rather than by several parties fighting against one another, (...)

The need for the Party to play a leading role in relation to the trade union movement stems from the existence of various interests in different regional, occupational and other groups; and this leading role constitutes a mechanism guaranteeing the possibility that these interests will be harmonised at the level of the interests of the working class as a single whole, and at the level of the interests of society in general.
Ideological and Educational Department of the Central Committee of the Polish United Workers Party

THE FREE TRADE UNION SONG

There are no free trade unionists today.
Wherever you turn, only private interest, money.
What has become of concern for the workers?
It has flown off to a far and distant land.
All that's left is careerism and status.
Worker be quiet! Shut your mouth!
You must work, even if for breaking your back
You're paid in trouble and sorrow.

If you want to be free
Join our ranks
With the free union, with the free union
With the free union, we'll live together.

Let's raise the flag of our ideals,
Let's carry it to our brothers,
It will change, it will change,
It will change what our life is made of!

The worker should take the helm of power
To change the face of the world
So that treachery and lies will cease
So that each will be a brother to all
And the worker's toil will be prized
Since his hands build up the country.
For labour and the common effort
Give us your hand, help us brother!

If you want to be free ... etc.

STRAJKUS (The Little Striker)

A new satirical journal from the Baltic coast. We have received an independent satirical journal from the coastal factories: it is called **Strajkus.** Here are some of the jokes in it.

SMALL ADS:
Workers of the world ... my sincere apologies! K. Marx.

Workers unite ... before it's too late! L. Walesa.

Workers unite ... freely, with Warsaw and the country. M. Jagielski (Deputy Premier) (1)

JOKE OF THE DAY:
PAP press agency announced today that work stoppages are still going on in certain factories in Gdansk-Gdynia-Sopot.

(1) The Polish verb means both "to unite" and "to get through" (on the phone)

Solidarity Strike Bulletin No.11 30 August 1980

REPRESSION IN ELBLAG

We have received the following report by a delegate from the factories on strike in Elblag.

On 21 August 1980, at 1915 hours, representatives of the Elblag MKS returning from Gdansk were arrested by the police at Adamowo and taken to the provincial police headquarters in Elblag. There someone from the political police, whose name is not known, questioned them about MKS activity in Gdansk and Elblag. He threatened to have them brought before the Kollegium (1) and the public prosecutor on a charge of transporting illegal written material. Some of their printed material was confiscated. Boguslaw Zakrzewski and Mieczyslaw Wolski were searched. Then it was suggested that they collaborate with the police, and they were offered money and a flat. Our delegates were only released after five hours' detention. In Pasklet, on the evening of 26 August 1980, a group of policemen who said they were looking for a thief, tried to break into the industrial construction enterprise, whose workers are on strike. The caretakers pointed out that the building was closed, and the police car parked for the whole night opposite the railings. There were no other incidents.

On 28 August, representatives of the PUWP provincial committee arrived at the PKS (motor-coach) enterprise, where the management was also to be found. One of these representatives, a man called Jamrozy, began to shout at and abuse engineer Hoffman, a member of the enterprise strike committee. He accused him of sowing ideological diversion: 'If you like the idea,' he said, 'you can stop work for six months.' In answer to the question: 'So, you will open fire on us?' he declared: 'If it's necessary, we'll shoot you!' While Jagielski, member of the PUWP Politbureau and vice-premier of the People's Republic of Poland, was discussing with the MKS, his Party comrades were trying to sow terror among the workers on strike. I ask the question: does the PUWP have two ways of dealing with strikers, the Jagielski way and the Jamrozy way?

When the Party representatives asserted that 90% of the coach workers want to go back to work, engineer Hoffman carried out an anonymous survey. Those who wanted the strike to continue had to write the letter 'S' on a small piece of paper, and those who wanted work to be resumed had to write the letter 'P'. The secret vote took place in the company shop. The result was 112 'S', 16 'P', and one abstention.

HOW SHOULD THIS TELEX BE UNDERSTOOD?

Mr Jagielski, the Deputy Premier, firmly stated during his discussions with the MKS that all the strikers will be fully compensated for the period of the strikes.

Basing ourselves on this statement, we understand that the telex originating from Piotr Karpiuk, deputy minister of Labour, Wages and Social Affairs, constitutes an illegal and arbitrary decision, taken independently of the higher authorities. We are convinced that people who take irresponsible decisions will immediately suffer the consequences. We print below the text of this telex message.

Telex dated 29 August 1980, sent by the director responsible for economic affairs at Warsaw CTHM (Technical Centre for Trade in Machine Tools) at 8.30 a.m.

'In conformity with the telex dated 28 August 1980 from Piotr Karpiuk — deputy minister of Labour, Wages and Social Affairs — and sent to Mejener — under-secretary of state at the Ministry of Metallurgy — concerning the remuneration of workers on strike:

1) It should be announced to the strike committees and workplace management that we agree to partial compensation for the wages of workers on strike.
2) The management will hold talks with the strikers to this effect.

3) Payment should take place immediately after the return to work.
4) Workers on strike have the right to remuneration according to their position on the wages grid. If the pay date fell during the strike, the strikers should be paid 40% of wages for the time of the work stoppage, according to their individual position.'

The above text was received by establishments in theprovinces of Gdansk, Elblag, Szczecin, Slupsk and Koszalin.

CTHM Director of Economic Affairs;
signed Eugeniusz Kolodziej.

HOW THE STRIKE BEGAN

Our reporter carried out a number of interviews with workers at the shipyards regarding the question of the beginning of the strike. Enclosed are two of them.

First Interview.

How did the strike begin?

We agreed with Bogdan that on 14 August we would arrive at work an hour early. We wanted to hang up a number of posters in the cloakrooms about the sacking of Anna Walentynowicz and demanding a wage increase of 1000 zlotys, together with a cost of living supplement. The posters with this information were made by the Movement of Young Poland. In total we had seven of them. I arrived first. Kajik arrived a little while later, with whom I had arranged the day before. Kajik works in Department W3. We went there first of all, where we hung the posters under the clocking-in clock, following which Kajik and a number of his mates stood around guarding the poster, so that no one would tear it down. In the meantime I went back to my department, where I waited for Bogdan. Because he was late I decided to begin on my own. I pasted up the posters and hung them on the doors of a cloakroom, and then went into other cloakrooms where I also hung them. While I was hanging the posters up people started congratulating me.

Did the people feel that there was likely to be a strike?

No, but previously we'd informed a small group of trusted people. But in the morning there was talk in the shipyards of a strike.

How did the people take this?

Very well. They asked us detailed questions. Small groups of people started to form meetings with the foremen. I started to inform them that the strike had begun in the whole shipyard and we were meeting outside in the square.

Did the foremen see the posters?

Yes, clearly. Everybody could see them. Even the management.

Did the management attempt to act against them in some way?

No, because around the posters groups of workers stood around, so management was frightened to intervene. Despite that the first fifteen minutes were rather tense. The foremen did attempt to intervene. So I went to one of the brigades where I knew some of the people and started to explain what we were fighting about. The majority agreed with me. At the request of the foremen, who had started to feel that something was about to happen, we moved away and started to group by the cloakroom. Soon a group of around 30 people formed up, with a similar sized group next to it, by the cloakroom. Fearing that this group might disperse I went up to them and started to explain about the strike. I explained that the whole shipyard was beginning the strike and that the question was an increase in pay and the matter of Mrs Walentynowicz, who had been thrown out of work unjustly. As I talked people began to gain in self-confidence.

'Let's go,' I said to them. Then a group of around 50 people moved out. We made a banner and just then the director, Barc, arrived and asked what the hell was going on. 'Director', I replied, 'we're on strike'. 'Why strike? Why? What's going on?' To which I replied, 'Can't you read?' and showed him the poster. I left him with a number of workers who had a declaration on the question of Anna. I went off trying to group other people. When I returned the Party Secretary of the department, Mazurkiewicz, had arrived and was attempting to take away the banner. But the lads were quicker than him and prevented him. The Secretary shouted, 'What's the meaning of this?', to which they replied 'none of your business'. Somebody shoved a number of leaflets into his hand, and everybody surrounded him and started to laugh, because it looked as if the Party Secretary was handing out leaflets. But I shouted at them to take them away, because I didn't want the leaflets to be found in such unworthy hands. When the Secretary left I picked up the banner and led the lads outside into the square. All this had occurred on the terrain of our department.

People were sitting around the square. Suddenly the Deputy

Director of the department, Bryczkowski, arrived. This mobilised people. They stood up and started to mill around in the centre of the square. Others joined them. When a large group had been formed a signal was given from a crane. It was a small siren put on for a joke. The Director started to get angry. 'What's going on? Go back to work!' he shouted. But nobody wanted to listen to him. Somebody shouted, 'Have a look at the banner and then you will know what is going on!' A locomotive arrived. It stopped beside us and the driver started to clap. With those formed up on the square we moved towards the hall of the prefabrication department. We waited there for about 5 minutes, when suddenly George and his group arrived. More and more people started to leave the hall. After a while the foremen arrived and started to push people back inside; but the whole of the hall had stopped work. People had left their hammers and were putting away their tools and joining us.

Second Interview

How did the strike begin?

I arrived at the shipyards at 4.15. Up until the day of the strike I hadn't told anybody that it was due to begin. In my department there was a majority of Party members and I was worried in case somebody informed the authorities and the strike would fail. I waited, therefore, till the last moment. On the day of the strike I arranged to meet Ludwig. I was the only one from the department. I hung up 7 posters and gave 5 to Ludwig. After doing that I arranged the leaflets, of which I had about 500, and gave one to everybody who entered, saying, 'Take one and read it. Today the whole shipyard is striking.'

Did the leaflet mention that today there was going to be a strike?

No, but I had asked the people I trusted the day before what they would do in the event of a strike. Many of them indicated that they would strike, and it was to those people I gave the leaflets, saying, 'Hand them out to other people'. At 5.45 the group formed up by the cloakrooms, about 30 people. Some of them were worried and started saying that the strike would fail; 'Why doesn't a larger department begin the strike?', to which I replied that departments K3 and K4 were already on strike. Then someone said, 'We're not standing here any longer. Let's go back to the hall.' I tried to stop this, but couldn't on my own. But I was aware that if they were to return to the hall where the foremen stood, where the First Secretary and member of the Central Committee Jan Labedzki was, everything could fail. People started to return to the machines and turn them on. I went up to them saying, 'Let's go to K3 and K4. They've both stopped.' It a shot in the dark because I wasn't certain that anything had happened yet... but I only wanted to get them to follow me.

At last the workers decided. 'O.K., let's go!' But even though they stopped the machines, they still hesitated. Finally, the urge to get out won the day. Thirty or so people gathered together and we left. I took the posters with me. We reached the canteen and then continued on our way throughout the shipyard. Everywhere people were coming out to see what was happening. We shouted to them: 'Leave your machines and come with us!' A good number did join us, and our now rather larger group crossed the bridge. People were coming off the ships. They had already stopped work, and yet they hesistated to join us. 'We're not working,' they said, 'but we can't join you yet.' It was obvious that they were afraid. We reached department K3, and there we saw a group of people gathered together. This boosted our morale: we were already sure of success, and shouted: 'Hurrah! Hurrah!' People working in the construction offices looked at us through the windows. A crowd was gathered outside, and we went with it to department K3.

A crowd? That's what, about 100 people?

Oh yes! I wanted someone to speak to the people. That would have fired them more, but we weren't in a hurry. We arrived with our banner at the far end of the shipyard, where the director, Wojcik, was already waiting. His first words were: 'What does this mean?' I answered: 'It's a strike!' 'What's it all about?' I said: 'The sacking of Anna Walentynowicz.' 'Anna Walentynowicz?' the director asked. 'You know who she is? She was sacked without notice. Someone like her: she has three order of merit decorations, one in bronze, one in silver and one in gold. She's got thirty years' work behind her, and she's only got five months before she retires.' The director started to move back. Bogdan said to him: 'We won't talk to you for the moment, sir.' We went on and left the director in the crowd. We put our men on the bridge to see that the road was not cut. A lot of people joined our demonstration. We arrived near the gate, where we observed a minute's silence in memory of the victims of 1970. Then we sang the national anthem. Then we went to the excavator, and after we climbed up it was immediately surrounded by the crowd. We gave a speech.

'We have to elect a strike committee. We need people we can trust, who have authority in the work brigades. Let them come forward.' Then the director appeared with his retinue. Since the director was beneath the excavator, we helped him to climb up. But when the director started to speak. Leszek Walesa suddenly appeared. The director didn't see him, for he had climbed on to the excavator from behind. Leszek went up to the director and asked him solemnly: 'Do you recognise me? I worked for ten years in the shipyard, and I still consider myself to be a docker. I have been given the trust of all the workers. It is already four years since I have been without a job.' And he continued, 'We shall hold a sit-in strike!'

At these words, loud hurrahs echoed everywhere. Afterwards, we asked that the director's car should bring Mrs Anna Walentynowicz back to the shipyard. The director protested, but we imposed our will and the director's car went off in search of Mrs Anna. As for us, we went off to the local transmitting centre. That is how the strike began.

SLUPSK IS WITH US!

The strike committee at the Sexamor naval equipment plant informs us that there is no MKS in Slupsk. We know, however, that all the public sector industrial enterprises are on a solidarity strike and have come out in support of the MKS at the Lenin shipyards in Gdansk.

WHO IS HIDING BEHIND IT?

Trybuna Ludu of 29 August published an article entitled: "Discussion and concern for the public good". Here is an extract from this irresponsible article:

"In Party meetings, and in discussions in Elblag and other places, it is said that the time has come to show one's cards, and to say who are the people leading the strike in Gdansk. It is also necessary to say who is hiding behind it."

Our answer: The strike leaders are workers and also Party members. Behind them are the worker masses, including many Party members. The strike committees are the work of the people demanding the right to its own tribune. For today the people has won solidarity.

NOTES

1) **Kollegium:** A collective body attached to the people's councils at every level of administration. It has the right to punish petty offences connected with administration and labour discipline.

ANDRZEJ WAJDA AT THE GDANSK SHIPYARDS

Andrzej Wajda, the distinguished Polish film director and author of the famous film **Man of Marble**, arrived today at the Gdansk shipyards. Profiting from the presence of the greatest creative artist of the Polish cinema, we asked him to say a few words for **Solidarity**.

You are the author of one of the best films about the situation of workers today. I am thinking of Man of Marble. **Nearly all the workers on strike know this film. It ends right here in the Gdansk shipyards. How do you view your film ten years later in the light of recent events?**

I have always dreamt of making a sequel to this filmI think I would be very happy if I managed to make a film recalling the history of the son of the hero in **Man of Marble**. In the meantime, you have written the story through your actions, of which the present events are the expression. That is why we already know what the film will be like. The story is already there, it has already taken place. Let's hope that it will end on a happy note, for its ending is the main concern for us all.

The action of Man of Marble **finished ten years ago. Today, as you point out, the hope expressed in the film is being accomplished. The actors in the current events are men who have never been 'men of marble'. Rather, they used to put flowers on their graves. It's as if they had changed their origin. The origin of the strike leaders. How do you view these men and the reasons behind their activity?**

I think that what is happening here is in a line of continuity with the past. I would like to make a sequel to the film, because I see that what we need most is a feeling of our own continuity. Nothing starts from square one: everything has roots in another time and another place. We did not just begin on Monday to be honest people; there were also honest people before. And even if they suffered defeats, or at least did not know success, it would not be good if we started again from scratch. That is why I would like to make a film that takes up where the other left off. I feel that in **Man of Marble** I succeeded in saying something true: I showed the profile of a worker who had his dignity, his ambition and his class consciousness. And so I would like to see what his son will be like. The fact that he is the son of a 'man of marble' is not without importance. I hope that he will not disappoint us; or in other words, that he will continue to defend his father's cause. I must say to you that I have only just arrived in the shipyard. I would like to look around and think about a lot of problems.

To end, then, we would like to ask you what are your first impressions of the shipyard.

The first impression is precisely the one that has reached us in Warsaw and other towns: an impression of calm, coolness, festivity, something lofty and extraordinary. I feel that I am witnessing a fragment of history — which does not happen often. In general history passes us by; but here you can feel it, see it, touch it.

Solidarity Strike Bulletin No.12 30 August 1980

ACTORS FROM THE WYBRZEZE (COAST) THEATRE VISIT THE GDANSK SHIPYARD STRIKERS

On 28, 29 and 30 August, in the meeting-hall used by the Inter-factory Strike Committee of the Gdansk shipyards, there was a performance in solidarity with the striking workers. Taking part were the following actors from the **Wybrzeze** theatre: J. Gorzko, M. Dworakowski, A. Blumenfeld, J. Kiszkis, J. Lapinski, A. Szacillo, S. Michalski, A. Nowinski, M. Pietrzyk, as well as accompanists H. Winiarska, E. Gociel, H. Slojewska, B. Czosnowska, H. Labonarska and A. Glowinska from the **Zak** theatre in Warsaw.

The spectacle was presented by Marciej Prus. The actors presented texts by, among others, Cz. Milosz, A. Mickiewicz, K.C. Norwid, J. Slowacki, K. Wierzynski, L. Dymarski, as well as anonymous creators of strike folklore.

More than a thousand spectators gave a very warm reception to the performance.

We would like to thank all the actors in the name of the strikers and the editors of **Solidarity.**
The Editors

A CALENDAR OF THE STRIKE

In this issue we are publishing the first part of a strike calendar drawn up by friends on the editorial board of **Robotnik.** The second part will be published in a coming issue of **Solidarity.**

Thursday, 14 August
6.00 a.m. Workers from departments K-1 and K-3 of the **Lenin** shipyard stopped work. In C-5 and the engine-construction department, the workers join in the strike. Groups of workers tour the shipyard holding banners that proclaim:
"We demand:
— the reinstatement of Anna Walentynowicz:
— a 1,000 zloty cost-of-living rise."

9.00 a.m. The meeting begins. Speeches are made; the workers sing. The strike is declared. A strike committee is formed. It presents the following demands:
— reinstatement of Anna Walentynowicz and Lech Walesa (members of the Coast Committee for the Creation of Free Unions, and of the December 1970 strike committee);
— building of a monument to the victims of December 1970;
— a guarantee that there will be no repression on account of the strike;
— a wage rise of 2,000 zlotys;
— linkage of family allowances to those paid to the police.

During the meeting, Lech Walesa climbed on to an excavator in the area of the shipyard hospital. From that time it is he who has led the strike.

The management accepts the demand to reinstate Anna Walentynowicz and to build a monument. It also undertakes to guarantee the strikers' security.

— Interpress (the press agency for foreign journalists) denies that a strike has broken out at the shipyards.
— In the evening, a Plenum of the PUWP Regional Committee meets in the presence of Politbureau member, Kania. In several contributions elements of hysteria can be detected. There is talk, for example, of "the terror established by the Inter-factory Strike Committee", of "anarchy" and "anti-socialist forces". Rear-admiral Janczyszyn declares that the army will do nothing that might loosen its bond with society.

Friday, 15 August
The strike spreads:
— to the **Paris Commune** shipyard in Gdynia. Here it is Andrzej Kolodziej who takes the head of the strike. He has only been working there for two days, having been dismissed from the Gdansk shipyard for distributing **Robotnik.**
— to virtually all the other shipyards;
— to the docks;
— to public transport;
— to enterprises connected with the shipbuilding industry.

At 12.00 p.m., telephone links with voivodship capitals are cut.

Talks go on all day with the management. On the latter's initiative, departmental representatives take part in the afternoon talks. Some of them are hesitant, undecided; some have been infiltrated by the management. This weakens the strikers' position.

The workers' militia has already been functioning for two days. It controls the entry-points so that no one from outside can get into the shipyard. It also makes sure that no one bring vodka in.

— The Committee of Social Self-defence — KOR publishes a declaration of solidarity with the strikers in which it protests against the severing of telephone links.

Saturday, 16 August
In the morning an ambulance is on stand-by. The management agrees to the wage rises. As for the other demands, it states that it does not have the competence to decide. The talks drag on, since the management refuses to give its promised written agreement to the wage rises. At about 3.00 p.m., Lech Walesa, in conformity with a majority vote, announces that the strike is over.

The strikers have won a 1,500-zloty wage rise and a so-called "docker's" cost-of-living bonus. After leaving the meeting-hall, Lech Walesa speaks with the workers and realises that an important number are for a continuation of the strike in solidarity with the workers in other enterprises, where the management has not even been prepared to make a promise. In light of this Lech Walesa cancels the decision to end the strike. But he cannot announce it, since the address system is not working from where he is.

Using the loud-speakers at his disposal, the director calls on the workers to leave the shipyard before 6.00 p.m. The majority of workers leave.

During the night, delegations arrive in the shipyard from 21 enterprises that are on strike. The Inter-factory Strike Committee is set up. It draws up a provisional list of demands. The workers who left the yard the previous evening begin to come back.
— PAP informs the country that the Baltic shipyard strike is over.

Sunday, 17 August
9.00 a.m. Inside the Gdansk shipyard, mass is celebrated before four to five thousand people (including workers from the repair shop), with another two thousand grouped togehter outside the gates. After mass, a cross is planted in front of No. 2 gate.

Monday, 18 August
— Those workers who left the shipyard are returning.
— The director denies the Inter-factory Strike Committee access to the internal radio. He also cuts off the electricity supply to the loudspeakers near gate no. 2, thereby depriving the hospital of electric current. The director broadcasts appeals for a return to work. An aeroplane drops leaflets calling for the strike to be halted.
— A meeting is held in front of the management offices. The director, Gniech, delivers a speech, but he is booed.

The Inter-factory Strike Committee already counts 156 enterprises; so the strike has become general. The committee presidium is enlarged so as to bring in eighteen new members.

At the request of the Gdansk and Gdynia shipyard strike committees, the civil authorities ban the sale of vodka in these two towns.
— The free press of Gdynia shipyard brings out an Inter-factory Strike Committee broadsheet addressed to the inhabitants of the Gdansk-Gdynia-Sopot agglomeration. It says: "The strike committees are keeping order in the workplaces. We shall hold out!"
– In a televised speech, Gierek rejects the workers' demands and expresses his agreement with the (official) Central Trade Union Council.
– The Committee of Social Self-defence – KOR and the editors of **Robotnik** launch an appeal to the workers of all Polish enterprises, inviting them to set up genuinely representative bodies: free trade unions.

Tuesday, 19 August
A delegation from the Inter-factory Strike Committee hands in a letter to Prime Minister Babiuch at the voivodship council building, in which the central authorities are asked to open negotiations.
— In the meantime, 17 enterprises (including the repair shop, and the "North" and "Wisla" shops), which belong to the MKS, begin separate negotiations with Pyka, the head of the government commission. A part of these delegations is made up of managers and first secretaries of Party cells.

— In a meeting at the Voivodship Council of the (official) unions, attended by representatives from 14 enterprises, the union president Szydlak declares: "We will not hand over power, and nor will we share it."

On the same day, the MKS numbers a membership of 253 enterprises.

Wednesday, 20 August
Under pressure from the workers, the strike committee delegates who had begun talks with Pyka break off separate negotiations. During the night, Pyka is relieved of his functions as head of the government commission.
— Intellectuals launch an appeąl for the recognition of the Inter-factory

Strike Committee. They ask both sides to show proof of moderation and common sense.
— Workers at the Polytechnic, the Opera and the Philharmonic bring their support to the strikers.
— The annoyances begin. Cars carrying delegates to their factories are stopped, searched and have their flags removed.(1)
— The press campaign against "anti-socialist forces" is stepped up.

The local press reports that a precondition of talks is the expulsion of KOR and the RMP (Young Poland Movement) from the strike movement.
— The police starts to arrest opposition militants. The government hopes that it will thereby "soften up" the MKS, believing that its firmness was inspired from outside.

— MKS statement: "...Our response to the anti-strike attitude of the Central Council of Trade Unions is to leave these unions, which are the property of the Party and government. This decision has been taken by all delegates representing the entirety of workers affiliated to the MKS."

In the same statement: "The strike committee of various enterprises should in no case deal with the state power concerning demands that are common to all the workers. We renew our appeal for talks to the government spokesman. By putting off such talks, it is cutting itself off from its own roots. As for us, we have been prepared to start talks since Saturday the sixteenth. The MKS is the only force capable of getting the workers' demands accepted by the government of the People's Republic of Poland."

Thursday, 21 August
— The government commission headed by vice-premier Mr Jagielski arrives in Gdansk. At 2.00 p.m. Jagielski proposes branch-by-branch discussions. Several attempts are made to pass over the head of the MKS: the vice-premier talks with "troikas" from various enterprises (the management, the secretary of the Party committee, and the president of the official union branch). These talks have no bearing on the situation.
— Every day, a crowd continues to come to the shipyard gates in order to hear the MKS communiques broadcast by the local transmitter.
— The dockers make a statement explaining that the day after the strike began, the government of the Polish People's Republic told Western ship-owners that since the strike was official, they had the right to demand compensation from their insurance companies.
— Jagielski speaks on the local radio station.
— The militia controls access to the shipyard, asking people who go in to show their papers.
— Work stops at the **Zamech** enterprise in Elblag. News of strikes in Slupsk and Ustka.
— MKS statement: "In connection with the intensification of false and provocative propaganda, the MKS declares: the strikers as a whole are not aiming to break the unity of the Polish nation, and are not acting in such a way as to harm the Polish state. If the government wishes to be convinced of the truth of our declarations, then it should come among the strikers, and get to know the decisions of the MKS, which is the strikers' only representative.
The truth should be sought here among us, and not in the building of the Voivodship People's Council."

After the attacks against "anti-socialist forces", Lech Walesa declared:

"No one is inspiring us, but I do know the KOR militants." Walesa then outlined the history of KOR.
— Having given up the idea of separate talks, delegates from the "North" and repair workshops are admitted to the MKS presidium.
— The night brings reports that preparations are being made to enter and destroy the Gdansk shipyard press.

Committee members therefore start to spend their nights in different shipyard departments.

Friday, 22 August
— The ministers of the government commission continue branch-by-branch talks with the "troikas". News of this is broadcast on the local radio.
— At 2.00 p.m. a MKS delegation goes to see Jagielski in his villa, and proposes that talks should be opened. The vice-premier accepts.
— Some intellectuals in Poznan give their support to the workers on strike.

In an appeal to the government, workers at Gdansk Univeristy call on the government to take the workers' interests into account.
— The government commission, headed by Barcikowski, begins talks with the Szczecin MKS, which presents a list of 36 demands, including one for the release of the KOR and **Robotnik** members.

Those factories to which the ministers proposed branch-by-branch discussions declare that they will enter into negotiations only through the medium of the MKS.

Saturday, 23 August
— Lech Walesa appeals for an end to the repression against supporters of the strike.
— 2.00 p.m. The Gdansk Voivodship Council arrives in the shipyard. It discusses with a four-person committee appointed by the MKS presidium (the proceedings are not transmitted by the local radio). Jagielski's arrival is fixed for 20.00 hours.

Sunday, 24 August
Leaflets signed by the WKFJN (Voivodship Front of National Unity) are distributed in the town. They accuse the MKS of refusing talks with the government commission "despite the invitation sent to it".
— The presidium meets with specialists who have come to the Gdansk shipyard. A specialist commission attached to the MKS is set up. Tadeusz Mazowiecki, editor-in-chief of the Catholic monthly **Wiez (The Link),** is appointed head of this commission.
— A delegation arrives from Szczecin. The two MKS consider that only an agreement on the formation of free trade unions — the first and central demand — can bring the strike to an end.
— In Warsaw, a plenum of the PUWP Central Committee is held.
— Important changes in the government and Party are announced. Gierek announces the modification of the trade-union law, and elections to the enterprise council.

Monday, 25 August
Given the lack of telephone links with the rest of the country, the MKS presidium calls for a vote on whether talks should be started with the government commission. The MKS delegations unanimously decide not to begin talks.
— In the evening, telephone links are re-established with Szczecin and

Warsaw, the MKS also secures a promise that debates within the shipyard will be broadcast by the local radio.
— In a communiqué, the Soviet press agency TASS mentions unease in the USSR at "western press interference in the internal affairs of Poland".

Tuesday, 26 August
Deputy Premier Jagielski, together with the government commission, arrives in the shipyard at 11.00 a.m. The two sides present their points of view during the talks. With regard to the first and most important of the list of demands, the MKS calls for the transformation of the strike committees into free trade unions at enterprise and voivodship level. It is precisely this demand which the government commission is not willing to accept. Jagielski proposes the appointment of a specialist group with participation from both sides, whose task will be to clarify points of view on the first demand.

— In a televised homily, the Primate of Poland, Cardinal Wyszynski calls for calm and reflection.

Wojna, editor of **Trybuna Ludu**, announces on television that the right to strike and a new press law might be introduced. He hints that the situation of the late 19th century cannot be repeated (a reference to the partition of Poland).

1)In the town and region of Gdansk, motor-car drivers were flying small Polish flags as a sign of their solidarity with the strikers.
— The strike bulletin **Solidarity** begins to be published by the free press of Gdansk shipyard. Issue number one includes the conventions of the International Labour Organisation concerning the right to strike and the right of association.
— The number of factories belonging to the MKS is already 388.

At 8.00 p.m., the government commission chaired by Deputy Premier Jagielski arrives in the shipyard. Talks begin with the MKS presidium. Lech Walesa presides over the discussions. Everything is relayed by the local transmitter. The talks mainly take up Jagielski's speech: the government has not re-established telephone links with other towns. As **Solidarity** put it, Jagielski's speech 'disappointed the audience because of its general character and its lack of concrete proposals. Mentioning the key demand for the creation of free unions independent of the Party, Mr Jagielski recognised that it was just for there to be an organisation effectively defending the workers' interests. The law currently in force has become inadequate and should be modified.' He also spoke of new elections to the enterprise councils (branches of the official unions). He refused to publish the MKS demands; and he omitted the question of the right to strike. He was astonished to learn that people associated with the strikers had been subjected to repression. He asserted that the Constitution upholds the freedoms of speech and publication, but that independent editions have a harmful and anti-socialist character. He assured everyone that there are no political prisoners in Poland.

MKS statement: "...Not a word is said about the existence of MKS in Gdansk, Szczecin and Elblag..." *(There follows the declaration which appeared in 'Solidarity' No.1.)*

Solidarity Strike Bulletin No.13 31 August 1980

THE REPRESSION

The Provincial Prosecutor's Office of the town of Warsaw, citing article 276/1 of the Penal Code, issued arrest warrants on 28 August against the following persons (the list is certainly not complete): Seweryn Blumsztajn, Miroslaw Chojecki, Ludwik Dornow, Mieczyslaw Grudzinski, Wieslaw Kecik, Jacek Kuron, Jan Litynski, Adam Michnik and Zbigniew Romaszewski. In addition, Jan Ajzner, Andrzej Bulc, Jan Cywinski, Stefan Kowalec, Sergiusz Kowalski, Wojciech Malicki and Henryk Wujec are already in prison on charges that are not known.

The police has also held people in the following towns:
Wroclaw: Aleksander Gleichgewicht, Prof. Miroslawa Chamcowna, Prof. Roman Duda, Dr Jan Waszkiewicz, R. Kolodziej, A. Lipinski.
Torun: Wieslaw Cichon, Marek Berek, Stanislaw Smigiel, Jan Szaja.
Krakow: Tomasz Ulianowicz, Wojciech Sikora, Stanislaw Wildstein, Andrej Mietkowski.

In **Wabrzezno**, Boleslaw Niklaszewski is in hospital in a critical condition after being arrested by the police. He has a ruptured spleen.
Andrzej Rumowski, a worker at the "North" shipyard currently doing his military service, has been on hunger strike in **Chelm Pomorski** since 20 August, in protest against the specific persecution to which he is subjected.

On 29 August in **Slupsk, the police arrested two representatives of the town committee of the oleographic industry, as well as Bogdan Grzesiuk.**

FROM THE CONFERENCE HALL

5.00 p.m. The Gdansk shipyard conference hall is full, even though the lull is growing longer before the decisive talks are started between the MKS and the government commission. It is full, even though this unconventional "meeting" is already in its sixteenth day and everyone is tired. Deputy Premier Jagielski is late; the MKS presidium appears in the hall. Lech Walesa takes the floor. He explains once again the significance of the agreement that has been reached, and goes on to spell out the details. He emphasises that the importance of the independent, self-managing unions will depend on the way in which they are governed and on the quality of the people around them. His speech is met with applause. The audience is excited and readily claps every speaker. Two questions stand out among numerous others:

1) Will the clause on the leading role of the PUWP within the state not limit the independence of the independent, self-managing unions?
2) Will such unions be created throughout the country? Or will they be confined to the Gdansk coast?

This question remains unclear. The temperature of the discussion mounts when questions are asked concerning the democratic militants currently in jail. The MKS position is clear and straightforward. They should be freed.

CALENDAR OF THE STRIKE (concluded)

Wednesday, 27 August
The strikes spread to the whole country. An Inter-factory Strike Committee is formed in Wroclaw. The strikers solidarise with the Gdansk MKS list of demands.

During the discussion between MKS representatives and specialists and the government commission, the strikers elaborate their demand that the strike committees should be transformed into a free trade-union founding committee.

Thursday, 28 August
In the official **Baltic Journal**, we read: "Nowhere in the world are there workers' organisations which are not linked to a definite political movement, or to an ideology and its party-political expression." The **Journal** asks which ideological orientation the free trade unions would represent. Here it is developing the government's idea that free trade unions are in contradiction with the Constitution of the People's Republic of Poland, since they would be independent of the Party. And the Constitution states that the Party is the leading force of the nation.

— The government delegation arrives with Jagielski at 11.00 a.m.

Discussion on the problem of censorship. The government commission points out that the Constitution guarantees freedom of expression. The MKS expresses its agreement with certain limitations enforced by the censorship. It emphasises, however, that stifling of the freedom of expression was one cause of the current crisis, and it asks for real guarantees that the various freedoms will be observed according to the law.

The MKS demands that the radios should broadcast mass once a week for the benefit of sick people. Jagielski considers that this is the province of the Church, not of the MKS.

Also dealt with is the problem of political prisoners and repression. The MKS makes a detailed intervention, but Jagielski gives evasive answers.

— During the break, Lech Walesa, standing near gate no. 2, appeals to all workers for solidarity, asking them to join the MKS but without stopping work.
— At 6.00 talks resume between the MKS and the government commission.

Money arrives from all over the country for the construction of a monument to the victims of December 1970.

Money also comes from the whole of Poland for MKS funds.

— There are now four MKS in the country: Gdansk (over 600 enterprises), Szczecin (over 200), Elblag (several dozen), Wroclaw (several dozen). Several key industrial enterprises are on strike: Papawag (railway coaches) in Wroclaw, the Dzierzynski and Marchlewski textile factories in Lodz, and so on. Public transport is on strike in a number of towns (Lodz, Wroclaw, Walbrzych, Slupsk, Koszalin). At Ursus (near Warsaw) a workers' solidarity committee has been set up.

Friday, 29 August
The government commission does not arrive at the appointed time. The negotiations start again at midday.

— A delegation arrives from several large enterprises in Lublin, Bytom, Wroclaw and other towns.

— Extract from a communique issued by the General Council of the Episcopate of Poland: "The Council expresses its gratitude to the workers on strike, as well as to their Committee and the government, for having avoided any disturbance to public order..."
— R. Ozek-Nowicki has sent 100,000 zlotys to the MKS, saying: "I owe this to my ancestors as well as to my comrades who fell on the field of honour."
— At 4.00 p.m., the Coast Theatre gives a performance.
— A delegation arrives from the Bydgoszcz MKS, which represents 32 enterprises.
— In a televised speech, Barcikowski speaks of "the enemies of socialism, of every stripe and every kind".

Saturday, 30 August
Gdansk Harbour Council announces that sixty people have been sent to Sowieszow for the harvest, which will provide food for the strikers.

— Delegations arrive from enterprises on strike in Slupsk and Lodz. In Slupsk the motor-coach workers (PKS) have decided to leave the official unions.

— At 10.30 a.m., talks resume between the government commission and the MKS presidium.
— Signature of the previously reached agreement — a document clarifying points of view on numbers one and two of the list of demands. Lech Walesa asks about the latest arrests in Warsaw, and calls on Jagielski to stop the arrests and release those already held.

Jagielski takes no position on the matter, and moves on to the draft of a joint MKS-government declaration on ending the strike and resuming work. The question of the draft is postponed. Mr Jagielski announces that he will return to Warsaw at about 8.00 p.m.
— At 4.00 p.m. the Drama Theatre begins a performance.
— A delegation arrives from seven enterprises on strike in Krosno Odrzanskie. A solidarity strike was organised there, with the threat that strike action would be renewed if the demands of the Baltic coast are not met.

— A delegation from Gdansk University announces that the enterprise council (i.e., the official union branch) has handed over its duties to the strike committee. They are in favour of university autonomy, among other things. The delegates thank R. Glebocki, in particular, for the help he has given.

— During the meeting, extremely heated discussions break out between the presidium and the MKS plenum. Discussion focuses on the independence of the new unions from the Party, and on their geographical spread. (There is a rumour that the formation of new unions only applies to the coast.) Also debated is the question of the jailed militants from the democratic opposition.

— The plenum decides to demand the release of all the political prisoners.
— A. Wielowiejski and Professor Stelmachowski refer to the disputed questions of the form and functioning of the new unions.
— Delegations arrive from Warsaw: from the enterprise council of Warsaw University, the **Warszawa** steel-works, **Teva** (which brings 76,340 zlotys collected by 5,000 workers), and the ZM Ursus Workers Solidarity

Committee. The last two have included among their demands the release of democratic opposition militants held in Warsaw. They name a list of the victims of repression.

Throughout the evening, discussions continue among the shipyard workers concerning points 1 and 2. Mr Jagielski does not arrive.

— The **Lenin** and **Katowice** steel-works, as well as some coal and copper mines, have threatened in their turn to begin a solidarity strike.

Solidarity Strike Bulletin (not numbered) 31 August 1980

Communiqué

At 5.00 p.m. on 30 August 1980, the government commission and the Gdansk MKS signed a final document confirming the agreement on the 21 demands presented by the strikers. The conclusion of this agreement has brought the strike to an end.

Deputy Premier Jagielski made a written commitment to have released before midday of tomorrow 1 September, those persons who have been arrested by the police in the course of the last two weeks, a list of whom has been sent by the MKS to the government commission.

Draft Statutes of the Independent, Self-Managed Union

CREATION AND NAME OF THE UNION

I. An occupational organisation of workers and employees (hereafter called simply workers) is created under the name Independent, Self-Managed Union (hereafter called simply union).

II. The union embraces workers of every occupation who accept the statutes.

III. 1) The bodies of the union are inter-factory strike committees (MKS) or strike committees if they are not affiliated to a MKS. At the moment when the union is constituted, the strike committees become union commissions or bureaux at the appropriate level.
2) In enterprises where no strike committee existed, the union bodies are formed by the workers who nominate constitutive committees. These committees declare their adhesion to MKS transformed into inter-enterprise union commissions.

IV. On the Gdansk coast, an inter-enterprise union organisation is created which embraces workers from the enterprises in this region. It includes those workers who were organised within the Gdansk MKS.

STATUTORY PRINCIPLES

I. Aims of the union and the means of achieving them.

The union has the following aims:

1) To satisfy the material, social and cultural needs of its members and their families, and to enable them to develop their occupational skills.
2) To guarantee the workers' economic and juridical interests with regard to their work, living conditions, safety and hygiene at work.
3) To attempt to bring the workers' interests into harmony with the functioning of the enterprise.
4) To develop democracy and solidarity in relations between workers.
5) To cultivate an active attitude among the workers for the good of the country and of all workers.

The union achieves its aims:

a) By representing its members before the employers, the authorities, the state administration, and the other organisations and institutions of society.
b) By affording legal aid and intervening in the case of conflict between a worker and the employer.
c) By organising and leading workers' protest actions when their interests are harmed — in particular, by declaring a strike when necessary.
d) By organising mutual aid among union members, and in particular by holding funds for assistance and loans.
e) By conducting socio-cultural activity, and by creating the conditions for rest after work.
f)By co-operating with the authorities and the state administration within the framework defined by law.

II. Structure and leadership of the union

1) **The circle:** the smallest cell of the union is the enterprise circle numbering at least ten persons. The circle is represented by an elected delegate.

2) **Enterprise organisations:** the enterprise organisation is the basic structure of the union. In large enterprises, there may exist intermediary levels in the form of department organisations. Several circles from different enterprises may form an inter-enterprise organisation. The enterprise organisation has the following bodies:
a) The membership assembly, and, in organisations with more than five hundred members, the assembly of delegates from the circles or department organisations.
b) The enterprise commissions (departmental or inter-enterprise), which are the day-to-day leadership and have the function of a bureau.
c) The control commissions.
Enterprise organisations may federate at regional level.

3) **Leading bodies of the union.** The union leadership is composed of:
a) The general assembly of delegates.
b) The bureau.
c) The control commission.
The general assembly comprises delegates from the enterprise organisations. Within the framework of the union, trade branches will also exist and embrace the workers in a single trade or in related trades.

III. Election principles

All leadership bodies at every level are elected. Elections take place every three years according to the following principles:
1) The number of candidates may not be restricted.
2) There will be a separate vote for each candidate (whichrules out restricted slates).
3) Voting is by secret ballot.
4) The chairperson is directly elected by the enterprise, department or inter-enterprise organisation, or by the general assembly of delegates, and not by the commission or elected bureau.
5) The same function may only be held for two terms.
6) Anyone holding a leadership function in the state administration, the economic apparatus or the bodies of a political organisation may not have responsibilities within the union.

IV. Creation of the union and voting on the statutes

Those who have taken part in drafting the statutes and have signed them, become founding members of the union. Other workers become members of the union from the moment when the enterprise commissions decide to accept them.

iii THE GDANSK AGREEMENT

Here we publish in full the historic agreement between the MKS and the Government ending the Gdansk strike on 31 August 1980.

(This protocol was signed on behalf of the strikers by Lech Walesa (President of the MKS), Andrzej Kolodziej and Bogdan Lis (Vice-Presidents), Mr and Mrs L. Badkowski, W. Gruszewski, A. Gwiazda, S. Izdebski, J. Kmiecik, Z. Kobylinski, H. Krzywonos, S. Lewandowski, A. Pienkowska, Z. Pzybylski, J. Sikorski, L. Sobieszek, T. Stanny, A. Walentynowicz, and F. Wisniewski.

It was signed for the Governmental commission by: President Mieczeslaw Jagielski (Vice Prime Minister), M. Zielinski, member of the Secretariat of the Central Committee of the PUWP, T. Fiszbach, President of the Party committee of Gdansk Voivod, and the Mayor of Gdansk, J. Kolodzieski.)

The governmental commission and the Inter-factory Strike Committee (MKS), after studying the 21 demands of the workers of the coast who are on strike, have reached the following conclusions:

— On Point No.1, which reads: 'To accept trade unions as free and independent of the party, as laid down in Convention No.87 of the ILO and ratified by Poland, which refers to the matter of trade union rights', the following decision has been reached:

1) The activity of the trade unions of People's Poland has not lived up to the hopes and aspirations of the workers. We thus consider that it will be beneficial to create new union organisations, which will run themselves, and which will be authentic expressions of the working class. Workers will continue to have the right to join the old trade unions and we are looking at the possibility of the two union structures co-operating.

2) The MKS declares that it will respect the principles laid down in the Polish Constitution while creating the new independent and self-governing unions. These new unions are intended to defend the social and material interests of the workers, and not to play the role of a political party. They will be established on the basis of the socialisation of the means of production and of the socialist system which exists in Poland today. They will recognise the leading role of the PUWP in the state, and will not oppose the existing system of international alliances. Their aim is to ensure for the workers the necessary means for the determination, expression and defence of their interests. The governmental commission will guarantee full respect for the independence and self-governing character of the new unions in their organisational structures and their functioning at all levels. The government will ensure that the new unions have every possibility of carrying out their function of defending the interests of the workers and of seeking the satisfaction of their material, social and cultural needs. Equally it will guarantee that the new unions are not the objects of any discrimination.

3)The creation and the functioning of free and self-governing trade unions is in line with Convention 87 of the ILO relating to trade union rights and Convention 97, relating to the rights of free association and collective negotiation, both of which conventions have been ratified by Poland. The coming into being of more than one trade union organisation requires changes in the law. The government, therefore, will make the necessary legal changes as regards trade unions, workers' councils and the labour code.

4) The strike committees must be able to turn themselves into institutions representing the workers at the level of the enterprise, whether in the fashion of workers' councils or as preparatory committees of the new trade unions. As a preparatory committee, the MKS is free to adopt the form of a trade union, or of an association of the coastal region. The preparatory committees will remain in existence until the new trade unions are able to organise proper elections to leading bodies. The government undertakes to create the conditions necessary for the recognition of unions outside of the existing Central Council of Trade Unions;

5) The new trade unions should be able to participate in decisions affecting the conditions of the workers in such matters as the division of the national asseta between consumption and accumulation, the division of the social consumption fund (health, education, culture), the wages policy, in particular with regard to an automatic increase of wages in line with inflation, the economic plan, the direction of investment and prices policy. The government undertakes to ensure the conditions necessary for the carrying out of these functions.

6) The enterprise committee will set up a research centre whose aim will be to engage in an objective analysis of the situation of the workers and employees, and will attempt to determine the correct ways in which their interests can be represented. This centre will also provide the information and expertise necessary for dealing with such questions as the prices index and wages index and the forms of compensation required to deal with price rises. The new unions should have their own publications.

7) The government will enforce respect for Article I, paragraph 1 of the trade union law of 1949, which guarantees the workers the right to freely come together to form trade unions. The new trade union will not join the **Central Council of Trade Unions (CRZZ). It is agreed that the new trade** union law will respect these principles. The participation of members of the MKS and of the preparatory committees for the new trade unions in the elaboration of the new legislation is also guaranteed.

THE RIGHT TO STRIKE

— On Point No.2, which reads: 'To guarantee the right to strike, and the security of strikers and those who help them', it has been agreed that:

The right to strike will be guaranteed by the new trade union law. The law will have to define the circumstances in which strikes can be called and organised, the ways in which conflicts can be resolved, and the penalties for infringements of the law. Articles 52, 64 and 65 of the labour code (which outlaw strikes) will cease to have effect from now until the new law comes into practice. The government undertakes to protect the personal security of strikers and those who have helped them and to ensure against any deterioration in their conditions of work.

FREEDOM OF EXPRESSION

— With regard to Point No.3, which reads 'To respect freedom of expression and publication, as upheld by the Constitution of People's Poland, and to take no measures against independent publications, as well as to grant access to the mass media to representatives of all religions', it has been added that:

1) The government will bring before the Sejm (Parliament) within three months a proposal for a law on control of the press, of publications, and of other public manifestations, which will be based on the following principles: censorship must protect the interests of the state. This means the protection of state secrets, and of economic secrets in the sense that these will be defined in the new legislation, the protection of state interests and its international interests, the protection of religious convictions, as well as the rights of non-believers, as well as the suppression of publications which offend against morality.

The proposals will include the right to make a complaint against the press-control and similar institutions to a higher administrative tribunal. This law will be incorporated in an amendment to the administrative code.

2) The access to the mass media by religious organisations in the course of their religious activities will be worked out through an agreement between the state institutions and the religious associations on matters of content and of organisation. The government will ensure the transmission by radio of the Sunday mass through a specific agreement with the Church hierarchy.

3) The radio and television as well as the press and publishing houses must offer expression to different points of views. They must be under the control of society.

4) The press as well as citizens and their organisations, must have access to public documents, and above all to administrative instructions and socio-economic plans, in the form in which they are published by the government and by the administrative bodies which draw them up. Exceptions to the principle of open administration will be legally defined in agreement with Point No. 3 para 1.

With regard to Point No.4 which reads: 'To re-establish the rights of people who were sacked after the strikes in 1970 and 1976 and of students who have been excluded from institutions of higher education because of their opinions, (b) to free all political prisoners, including Edmund Zadrozynski, Jan Kozlowski and Marek Kozlowski; (c) to cease repression against people for their opinions;' it has been agreed:

(a) to immediately investigate the reasons given for the sackings after the strikes of 1970 and 1976. In every case where injustice is revealed, the person involved must be re-instated, taking into account any new qualifications that person may have acquired. The same principle will be applied in the case of students.

(b) The cases of persons mentioned under point (b) should be put to the Ministry of Justice, which within two weeks will study their dossiers. In cases where those mentioned are already imprisoned, they must be released pending this investigation, and until a new decision on their case is reached.

(c) to launch an immediate investigation into the reasons for the arrests of those mentioned (the three named individuals).
(d) to institute full liberty of expression in public and professional life.

On Point No.5, which reads: 'To inform the public about the creation of the MKS and its demands, through the mass media', it has been decided that:
This demand shall be met through the publication in all the national mass media of the full text of this agreement.

On Point No.6, which reads: 'To implement the measures necessary for resolving the crisis, starting with the publication of all the relevant information on the socio-economic situation, and to allow all groups to participate in a discussion on a programme of economic reforms', the following has been agreed:
We consider it essential to speed up the preparation of an economic reform. The authorities will work out and publish the basic principles of such a reform in the next few months. It is necessary to allow for wide participation in a public discussion of the reform. In particular the trade unions must take part in the working out of laws relating to the enterprises and to workers' self-management. The economic reform must be based on the strengthening, autonomous operation and participation of the workers' councils in management. Specific regulations will be drawn up in order to guarantee that the trade unions will be able to carry out their functions as set out in Point No.1 of this agreement.

Only a society which has a firm grasp of reality can take the initiative in reforming the economy. The government will significantly increase the areas of socio-economic information to which society, the trade unions and other social and economic organisations have access.

The MKS also suggests, in order that a proper perspective be provided for the development of the family agricultural units, which are the basis of Polish agriculture, that the individual and collective sectors of agriculture should have equal access to the means of production, including the land itself, and that the conditions should be created for the recreation of self-governing co-operatives.

On Point No.7, which reads: 'To pay all the workers who have taken part in the strike for the period of the strike as if they were on paid holiday throughout this period, with payment to be made from the funds of the CRZZ', the following decision has been reached:
Workers and employees participating in the strike will receive, on their return to work, 40% of their wages. The rest, which will add up to a full 100% of the normal basic wage, will be calculated as would holiday pay, on the basis of an 8-hour working day. The MKS calls on workers who are members to work towards the increase of output, to improve the use of raw materials and energy, and to show greater work discipline, when the strike is over, and to do this in cooperation with the management of the factories and enterprises.

On Point No.8, which reads: 'To increase the minimum wage for every worker by 2000 zlotys a month to compensate for the increase in prices', the following has been decided:

These wage increases will be introduced gradually, and will apply to all types of workers and employees and in particular to those who receive the lowest wages. The increases will be worked out through agreements in individual factories and branches. The implementation of the increases will take into account the specific character of particular professions and sectors. The intention will be to increase wages through revising the wage scales or through increasing other elements of the wage.

White collar workers in the enterprises will receive salary increases on an individual basis. These increases will be put into effect between now and the end of September 1980, on the basis of the agreements reached in each branch.

After reviewing the situation in all the branches, the government will present, by 31 October 1980, in agreement with the trade unions, a programme of pay increases to come into effect from 1 January 1981 for those who get the least at the moment, paying particular attention to large families.

On Point No.9, which reads: 'To guarantee the sliding scale', the following decision has been reached:
It is necessary to slow down the rate of inflation through stricter control over both the public and private sectors, and in particular through the suppression of hidden price increases.

Following on from a government decision, investigations will be carried out into the cost of living. These studies will be carried out both by the trade unions and by scientific institutions. By the end of 1980, the government will set out the principles of a system of compensation for inflation, and these principles will be open to discussion by the public. When they have been accepted, they will come into effect. It will be necessary to deal with the question of the social minimum in elaborating these principles.

On Point No.10, which reads: 'To ensure the supply of products on the internal market, and to export only the surplus', and Point No.11, which reads: 'To suppress commercial prices and the use of foreign currency in sales on the internal market', and Point No.12, which reads: 'To introduce ration cards for meat and meat-based products, until the market situation can be brought under control', the following agreement has been reached:
The supply of meat will be improved between now and 31 December 1980, through an increase in the profitability of agricultural production and the limitation of the export of meat to what is absolutely indispensable, as well as through the import of extra meat supplies. At the same time, during this period a programme for the improvement of the meat supply will be drawn up, which will take into account the possibility of the introduction of a rationing system through the issue of cards.

Products which are scarce on the national market for current consumption will not be sold in the 'Pewex' shops; and between now and the end of the year, the population will be informed of all decisions which are taken concerning the problems of supply.

The MKS has called for the abolition of the special shops and the levelling out of the price of meat and related products.

 On Point No.13, which reads: 'To introduce the principle of cadre selec-

tion on the basis of qualifications, not on the basis of membership of the party, and to abolish the privileges of the police (MO) and the security services (SB), and of the party apparatus, through the abolition of special sources of supply, through the equalisation of family allowances, etc.', we have reached the following agreement:
The demand for cadres to be selected on the basis of qualifications and ability has been accepted. Cadres can be members of the PUWP, of the SD (the Democratic Party, which draws its membership from small private enterprises), of the ZSL (the Peasant Party — these three parties make up the National Front) or of no party. A programme for the equalisation of the family allowances of all the professional groups will be presented by the government before 31 December 1980. The governmental commission states that only employees' restaurants and canteens, such as those in other work establishments and offices, are operated...

On Point No.14, which reads: 'To allow workers to retire at 50 years for women and 55 for men, or after 30 years of work for women, and 35 years for men, regardless of age', it has been agreed that:
The governmental commission declares pensions will be increased each year taking into account the real economic possibilities and the rise in the lowest wages. Between now and 1 December 1981, the government will work out and present a programme on these questions. The government will work out plans for the increase of old age and other pensions up to the social minimum as established through studies carried out by scientific institutions; these will be presented to the public and submitted to the control of the trade unions.

The MKS stresses the great urgency of these matters and will continue to raise the demands for the increase of old age and other pensions taking into account the increase of the cost of living.

On Point No.15, which reads: 'To increase the old-style pensions to the level paid under the new system', it has been agreed:

The governmental commission states that the lowest pensions will be increased every year as a function of rises in the lowest wages. The government will present a programme to this effect between now and 1 December 1981. The government will draft proposals for a rise in the lowest pensions to the level of the social minimum as defined in studies made by scientific institutes. These proposals will be presented to the public and subject to control by the unions.

On Point No. 16, which reads: 'To improve working conditions and the health services so as to ensure better medical protection for the workers', it has been agreed that:
It is necessary to immediately increase the resources put into the sphere of the health services, to improve medical supplies through the import of basic materials where these are lacking, to increase the salaries of all health workers, and with the utmost urgency on the part of the government and the ministries, to prepare programmes for improving the health of the population. Other measures to be taken in this area are put forward in the appendix.

On Point No. 17, which reads: 'To ensure sufficient places in creches and play schools for the children of all working women', it has been agreed that:
The governmental commission is fully in agreement with this demand.

The provincial authorities will present proposals on this question before 30 November 1980.

On Point No. 18, which reads: 'To increase the length of maternity leave to 3 years to allow a mother to bring up her child', it has been decided that:
Before 31 December 1980, an analysis of the possibilities open to the national economy will be made in consultation with the trade unions, on the basis of which an increase in the monthly allowance for women who are on unpaid maternity leave will be worked out.

The MKS asks that this analysis should include an allowance which will provide 100% of pay for the first year after birth, and 50% for the second year, with a fixed minimum of 2,000 zlotys a month. This goal should be gradually reached from the first half of 1981 onwards.

On Point No. 19, which reads: 'To reduce the waiting period for the allocation of housing', the following agreement has been reached:
The district authorities will present a programme of measures for improving the accommodation situation and for reducing the waiting list for receipt of accommodation, before 31 December 1980. These proposals will be put forward for a wide-ranging discussion in the district, and competent organisations, such as the Polish town-planners association, the Central Association of Technicians etc. will be consulted. The proposals should refer both to ways of using the present building enterprises and prefabricated housing factories, and to a thoroughgoing development of the industry's productive base. Similar action will be taken throughout the country.

On Point No.20, which reads: 'To increase the travelling allowance from 40 to 100 zlotys, and to introduce a cost-of-living bonus', it has been agreed that:

An agreement will be reached on the question of raising the travelling allowance and compensation, to take effect from 1 January 1981. The proposals for this to be ready by 31 October 1980.

On Point No.21, which reads: 'To make Saturday a holiday. In factories where there is continuous production, where there is a four-shift system, Saturday working must be compensated for by a commensurate increase in the number of holidays, or through the establishment of another free day in the week', it has been agreed that:
The principle that Saturday should be a free day should be put into effect, or another method of providing free time should be devised. This should be worked out by 31 December 1980. The measures should include the increase in the number of free Saturdays from the start of 1981. Other possibilities relating to this point are mentioned in the appendix, or appear in the submissions of the MKS.

After reaching the above agreements, it has also been decided that:
The Government undertakes:
— to ensure personal security and to allow both those who have taken part in the strike and those who have supported it to return to their previous work under the previous conditions;

— to take up at the ministerial level the specific demands raised by the workers of all the enterprises represented in the MKS;
— to immediately publish the complete text of this agreement in the press, the radio, the television, and in the national mass media.

The strike committee undertakes to propose the ending of the strike from 5.00 pm on 31 August 1980.

STRAJKOWY BIULETYN INFORMACYJNY

ŻĄDANIA STRAJKUJĄCYCH ZAŁÓG

zakładów pracy i przedsiębiorstw reprezentowanych przez Międzyzakładowy Komitet Strajkowy

Międzyzakładowy Komitet Strajkowy reprezentuje również załogi zakładów pracy i instytucji, których funkcjonowanie jest niezbędne społecznie. Komitet ów ma na celu doprowadzić do rozmów, które spełnią oczekiwania strajkujących załóg.

Jednym z pierwszych warunków rozpoczęcia rozmów jest odblokowanie wszystkich telefonów.

Żądania strajkujących załóg reprezentowanych przez Międzyzakładowy Komitet Strajkowy są następujące:

1. Akceptacja niezależnych od partii i pracodawców wolnych związków zawodowych, wynikająca z ratyfikowanej przez PRL Konwencji nr 87 Międzynarodowej Organizacji Pracy dotyczącej wolności związkowych.
2. Zagwarantowanie prawa do strajku oraz bezpieczeństwa strajkującym i osobom wspomagającym.
3. Przestrzegać zagwarantowaną w Konstytucji PRL wolność słowa, druku i publikacji, a tym samym nie represjonować niezależnych wydawnictw oraz udostępnić środki masowego przekazu dla przedstawicieli wszystkich wyznań.
4. a) Przywrócić do poprzednich praw:
   —ludzi zwolnionych z pracy po strajkach w 1970 i 1976 r.
   —studentów wydalonych z uczelni za przekonania.
   b) Uwolnić wszystkich więźniów politycznych (w tym Edmunda Zadrożyńskiego, Jana Kozłowskiego i Marka Kozłowskiego).
   c) Znieść represje za przekonania.
5. Podać w środkach masowego przekazu informację o utworzeniu się Międzyzakładowego Komitetu Strajkowego oraz opublikować jego żądania.
6. Podjąć realne działania mające na celu wyprowadzanie kraju z sytuacji kryzysowej poprzez:
   a) podawanie do publicznęj wiadomości pełnej informacji o sytuacji społeczno-gospodarczej
   b) umożliwienie wszystkim środowiskom i warstwom społecznym uczestniczenia w dyskusji nad programem reform.
7. Wypłacić wszystkim pracownikom biorącym udział w strajku wynagrodzenie za okres strajku jak za urlop wypoczynkowy z funduszu CRZZ.
8. Podnieść wynagrodzenie zasadnicze każdego pracownika o 2000 zł na miesiąc jako rekompensatę dotychczasowego wzrostu cen.
9. Zagwarantować automatyczny wzrost płac równolegle do wzrostu cen i spadku wartości pieniądza.
10. Realizować pełne zaopatrzenie rynku wewnętrznego w artykuły żywnościowe a eksportować tylko i wyłącznie nadwyżki
11. Znieść ceny komercyjne oraz sprzedaż za dewizy w tzw. eksporcie wewnętrznym.
12. Wprowadzić zasady doboru kadry kierowniczej na zasadach kwalifikacji a nie przynależności partyjnej oraz znieść przywileje MO, SB i aparatu partyjnego poprzez:
    —zrównanie zasiłków rodzinnych
    —zlikwidowanie specjalnych sprzedaży, itp.
13. Wprowadzić na mięso i przetwory kartki - bony żywnościowe (do czasu opanowania sytuacji na rynku).
14. Obniżyć wiek emerytalny dla kobiet do 50 lat a dla mężczyzn do lat 55 lub przepracowanie w PRL 30 lat dla kobiet i 35 lat dla mężczyzn bez względu na wiek.
15. Zrównać renty i emerytury starego portfela do poziomu aktualnie wypłacanych.
16. Poprawić warunki pracy Służby Zdrowia, co zapewni pełną opiekę medyczną osobom pracującym.
17. Zapewnić odpowiednią ilość miejsc w żłobkach i przedszkolach dla dzieci kobiet pracujących.
18. Wprowadzić urlop macierzyński płatny przez okres trzech lat na wychowanie dziecka.
19. Skrócić czas oczekiwania na mieszkanie.
20. Podnieść diety z 40 zł do 100 zł i dodatek za rozłąkę.
21. Wprowadzić wszystkie soboty wolne od pracy. Pracownikom w ruchu ciągłym i systemie 4-brygadowym brak wolnych sobót zrekompensować zwiększonym wymiarem urlopu wypoczynkowego lub innymi płatnymi dniami wolnymi od pracy.

Międzyzakładowy Komitet Strajkowy

Wolna drukarnia Stoczni Gdynia
druk bezpłatny

Gdańsk, dnia 22 sierpnia 1980 r.

Gdansk strike leaflet dated 22 August, listing the 21 demands.

iv DOCUMENTS FROM SZCZECIN, KATOWICE & GDYNIA

Here we publish key documents from two other key centres of the August strike movement, Szczecin on the North West Coast by the East German border and Katowice in the South West near the Czechoslovak border.

The Szczecin workers began their strike four days after the Gdansk workers and reached agreement with the government just before the signing in Gdansk. The workers in the Katowice area erupted into a huge strike three days before the Gdansk settlement and played a big part in forcing the government to settle quickly in the North.

The shipyard workers in Szczecin began their strike on 18 August at 11am in the Warski yard and the strike then spread to the Parnic yard before reaching out to other sections of the working class in the city.

We print below three consecutive sets of demands from the shipyards: first, the initial set of demands presented by the 43-person elected strike committee of the Warski yard representing 35 sections. These demands were presented to the secretary of the provincial Party committee, Brych, who came to meet the strikers. When he denied the existence of political prisoners he was heckled and the meeting broke up; the second set of demands was drawn up in a declaration from the Parnic yard strike committee; and the third and longest list of demands was the platform of the united strike committee of the shipyard workers, drawn up after the other two.

Then follows the text of the Szczecin agreement, and the text of the Katowice agreement.

WARSKI YARD DEMANDS

From 1100 hrs on 18 August a strike has been in progress at the Warski Shipyard in Szczecin. At 0600 hrs a strike began at the Parnic Shipyard. In both shipyards a strike committee was formed and they have been in contact with each other.

There are 41-43 persons in the Warski Shipyard Strike Committee who represent 35 sections. The demands of the strikers are:

—clarification of the political and economic situation
—release of political prisoners
—the formation of free trade unions

—the erection of a monument commemorating the victims of the events of 1970
—a wage increase of 2000 zlotys
—a lowering of the retirement age of workers in especially demanding occupations
—a number of other demands similar to those put forward in Gdansk.

The demands were presented at a meeting to the Secretary of the provincial Party organization, Brych. When he denied the existence of political prisoners he was heckled and the meeting broke up.

PARNIC YARD DEMANDS

1. The work force supports the workers' strikes in Poland.
We demand:
2. A wage increase of 2000 zlotys, plus 1000 because of price increases.
3. Saturdays off with full pay.
4. An equalization of social benefits with those of the police and army.
5. Abolition of special shops for the army, police and Party.
6. The right to strike.
7. The formation of free trade unions.
8. The Party and the CZRR are responsible for the situation in Poland.
9. The abolition of censorship.
10. Full freedom for the church.
11. Reliable information on Poland.
12. A guarantee to be given in the evening news of the declaration of human rights signed in Helsinki.
13. The dissemination of news about the strikes and their demands in the press, radio and television.
14. An improvement in medical services and in the availability of medicine.
15. An increase in pensions and a reduction in the retirement age to 50 for women and 55 for men.
16. A general improvement in the availability of consumer goods in the country.
17. Abolition of limits on the wages fund. A division of the fund according to productivity.
18. A full guarantee that the presented demands be carried out.

Aleksander Krystosiak has been delegated to represent the shipyard.

SZCZECIN JOINT DEMANDS

We demand a telephone connection with the strike committee of the Gdansk shipyard.

1. The formation of trade unions which would be free and independent of the government and Party, and the creation of conditions which would permit them to function independently.
2. We demand improvement in the supply of food and consumer goods on the market.
3. We demand a wage increase of 2000 zlotys.
4. A raise in the minimal pension and disability payments to 3000 zlotys.
5. Workers who have suffered ill health as a result of their work to obtain incomes not lower than what they had at their previous place of work.
6. We demand family subsidies, pensions and disability payments to be on a par with those received by the army and police.
8. To distribute the declaration on human rights from the Helsinki Accords in printed form.
9. To legalize the right to strike in the constitution of the Polish Peoples Republic.
10. We demand a guarantee that neither the strikers nor especially their elected leaders will be subject to persecution.
11. To stop persecuting the activists of the opposition and to permit the formation of new political and social groups.
12. We demand complete freedom of activity for the Catholic Church's work in Poland, and the broadcasting of the mass on radio and television on Sundays and holy days.
13.To finance the erection of a commemoratory plaque in front of the shipyard's gates in memory of the victims of the events of December 1970.
14. That financing of totally unnecessary projects such as astronauts and aid to the Third World be terminated.
15. We demand an improvement in medical facilities and services in Poland and especially a satisfactory supply of medicine (to be available on the market) at prices comparable to what the police and army personnel pay.
16. To stop price rises and to increase price controls on services in both the private and state sector.
17. To abolish the special shops for the Party, police and army.
18. To abolish the (so-called) commercial shops as well as (so-called) commercial and express prices.
19. We demand that the sale of special Polish products at the PEWEX shops be stopped.
20. We demand an explanation of the present situation in the country, and that those responsible for it should suffer the consequences.
21. Stop secret price rises.
22. We demand that the shipyard be better supplied with the materials needed for production.
23. That the people involved in the workers' committees in 1970 have the right to work, and that they be accepted for work.
24. Terminate censorship in the Polish Peoples' Republic.
25. We demand that all workers have paid Saturdays off.
26. We demand that the government solve the housing shortage and guarantee that the waiting list for housing be not longer than 5 years.

27.To limit compulsory military service to one year and that the second year of national service be spent in a branch of the national economy.
28. That workers be demoted if they cannot fulfil their jobs as foremen or managers, and not shifted to similar positions as has hitherto been the case.
29. To review superfluous white-collar jobs and to abolish manual jobs held by intellectuals.
30. To amalgamate the TK with the shipyard and thus rationalize the administration.
31. To increase the amount of travelling expenses given to employees travelling on enterprise business.
32. To stop sending employees to Party schools at the cost of the enterprise.
33. To combine the shipyard workers' card with the miners' card.
34. To give other workers temporarily working for the shipyard the same rights as those with shipyard workers' cards.
35. Payment for the time on strike to be paid from the trade union fund which comes from the membership dues.
36. To print the striking shipyard workers' demands in the press.

THE SZCZECIN AGREEMENT

(The settlement between the strike committee in Szczecin and the government was published in Szczecinski Kurier. *The English translation appeared in* The Times *on 1 September 1980.)*

1. Creation of self-managing trade unions of a socialist character according to the Polish constitution. Strike committees would become new workers commissions and would prepare elections to the new trade unions.

2. A special government programme to be carried out by December 31 on prices and availability of supplies.

3. Pay rises to be granted, with emphasis on the lowest paid workers.

4. Retirement benefits to be raised by January 1, 1981.

5. Workers disabled at work to get the same pay even if forced to take a lower-paid job.

6. Women with babies may stay at home for three years, as under the present law, but will be compensated during the entire period.

7. Family allowances to be raised to the same level as militia and army family allowances and be received in three instalments, the first on January 1, 1981.

8. Final Act of the Helsinki Accords to be published as well as the United Nations Charter on Human Rights.

9. No prosecutions against workers for strike activities.

10. No reprisals against political activists if they do not violate 'socialist principles'.

11. Dialogue between the Church and state to be expanded and more access for the church to the news media.

12. Construction of a marble plaque to commemorate workers killed in the 1970 rioting at the Szczecin shipyard.

13. Health service in Poland to be improved and better supplies of medicines guaranteed.

14. An end to 'silent' price rises for basic goods.

15. Distribution of foodstuffs equally in all stores without favouritism.

16. An increase in meat supplies.

17. No Polish goods to be sold in hard currency shops unless supplies more adequate in shops for the Polish public (especially ham, which is often sold only in hard currency stores).

18. The strike situation to be explained to the Polish people.

19. More raw materials for enterprises.

20. Those who lost jobs because of strike activity between 1970 and 1980 to be reemployed after case-by-case study.

21. A special study of censorship to be completed by November 30.

22. The issue of making Saturday, normally a working day, an extra day off to be settled by December 31.

23. Reduction in the maximum waiting time for housing from the present 12 years to 5 years.

24. Holiday allowance to be increased by the end of the year.

25. Trade unions to be given the right to delegate workers to special educational programmes involving advanced studies.

26. Workers to get 40 per cent of their wages while on strike.

27. Shipyard workers' charter to be modified by the end of the year.

28. The agreement to be published by the local media and the national press agency.

THE KATOWICE AGREEMENT

Agreement concluded by a Government commission formed according to Order No 39 of 9 September 1980. Agreement between the Council of Ministers and the workers' committee which is currently based in the Katowice steel mill, concerning a guarantee that the agreement concluded between the MKS and the Government Commission on 31 August 1980 will be implemented.

The guarantee that the conditions of the Gdansk agreement of 31 August 1980 concerning the autonomous and independent trade unions, referred to hereafter as the Independent Unions, will be carried out is based on the understanding that neither the police, the secret police nor the local management will interfere with the founding organisation and the functioning of these unions, and that the Independent Unions will fulfill the formalities stipulated in the new law from the moment it comes into force. This guarantee involves:

1. Time off work for persons engaged in the functioning of the Independent Unions, with pay for the time spent on these functions at the rates set down in existing regulations concerning trade union counsels.

2. Facilities must be made available by local factories for the use of local branches of the Independent Unions, and by the state for the use of the higher organs of the Independent Unions.

3. The dissemination of information about the activities of the Independent Unions in the press, radio and television on a scale commensurate with their size and importance; as well as access to the mass media for the representatives of the Independent Unions.

4. That local management assures the local branches of the Independent Unions of a say in all decisions regarding social matters previously dealt with by the trade unions, as well as in all matters of hiring, remuneration and dismissal of its members within the limits which the law will set to the operation of the Independent Unions in such matters.

5. The opening of accounts in local branches of the State Bank for membership dues of the members of the local branches of the Independent Unions.

6.An assurance that until new regulations concerning loans and benefits for workers have been established, a change in trade-union membership will not lead to any persons, using these services in a manner not in accord with existing regulations, suffering any penalties.

7. It has been decided that before the laws on trade unions and on the formation of the Independent Trade Union formed by the MKR with its temporary headquarters in the Katowice steel mills are implemented, the Party Secretary of Katowice province will be informed. Together with the statute, a list of the Union's leaders and a decision on a site will be presented. Local branches of the Independent Trade Union outside Katowice province have the right to establish contact with local state administration.

8. The Independent Trade Unions will be guaranteed a say in the formation of new laws on trade unions, workers' self-management, and on the revision of the labour code, ie. consultations, opinions, participation in commissions.

9. An assurance of freedom of activity and security for the members of the MKR based presently at the Katowice steel mill, and for the local workers' committees represented by the Committee (MKR), as well as for:
— persons helping the MKR and local committees
— all strikers
— the families of the above persons.

These decisions are compulsory for all state organs and local managers, at present as well as in the future. The harassment under a legal guise of the above persons and their families is forbidden. These decisions include a guarantee of full personal security and immunity, especially for the individuals in the MKR with its temporary headquarters at the Katowice steel mill. These guarantees refer to the activities mentioned in this agreement.

The Independent Trade Unions will attempt to cooperate with management to raise productivity and to mobilize the work force in order to realize economic objectives as well as possible.

The leader of the MKR
Andrzej Rozplochowski

The leader of the
Government Commission
Franciszek Kaim
Minister of Mining

Signatures follow:

From the MKR (Inter-factory Workers' Committee):
Jacek Jagielka, deputy-leader; Bogdan Barkowski, deputy-leader; Kazimierz Switon, secretary; Aleksander Karpierz, Zbigniew Kupsiewicz, and Wieslaw Tatko, members of the committee.

From the Government Commission:
Kazimierz Sada, secretary of the Ministry of Mining and director of the ZMZ; Zbigniew Szalajda, director of the Katowice steel mill; Eugeniusz Pustowka, director of the Lenin steel mill; Antoni Seta, leader of the ZG; Franciszek Grzesiak, General director of non-ferrous metals; and Michal Stepnial, director of the department of labour and wages in the Ministry of Mining.

Katowice Steel Mill **11 September 1980**

INTERVIEW WITH TWO GDYNIA WORKERS —By Ewa Barker

How did the strike in the Gdynia shipyard start and how did you make contact with the strike committee in the Lenin Shipyard in Gdansk?

The strike started spontaneously on Friday after the power supply to the shipyard had been cut off. We do not know who ordered the power cut; in any case, the order came from outside. And that was immediately taken as a call to strike. People were dissatisfied because of food shortages and rising prices. Besides, we'd already heard the day before that there was a strike in the Gdansk shipyard.

The workers left their posts and headed towards the directors' building. When about 300 people had gathered in front of the gates of the building the first demands were made. We demanded that the directors allow us to use the PA system so that we could organize ourselves and inform everyone of the situation. When this demand was met we asked for an increase in wages like the Gdansk shipyard workers. Our next problem was to get rid of those who opposed the strike, that is, the directors and heads of departments (a department has from 500-1,500 members) and the shop stewards of the old unions (they had sided with the directors rather than the strikers and still do so.) We did this by shutting them in separate rooms or by escorting them outside the gates.

We'd learned our lesson from the strikes of 1970 and decided to occupy the yards and definitely not go out on the streets. We placed guards around the shipyard.

On Saturday we sent two representatives to the shipyard in Gdansk so that we could coordinate action. Sunday, the third day of the strike, was crucial because we had heard that the Gdansk shipyard had signed an agreement and called off the strike, and up till then we received **nothing** from the authorities. However, on Sunday evening the Joint Strike Committee was organized (MKS). The MKS worked out 21 demands to place before the authorities and asked for support from other workers on the Baltic coast. Various services essential to the Functioning of daily city life were deliberately exempted from taking an active part in the strike. These included the health service, local electric train service, power stations and shops. Workers in the services, at the same time, declared their support for the strike.

How was the Strike Committee set up?

A Strike Committee was set up on the first day of the strike by Andrzej Kolodziej. He asked for people to help him. It was mostly young people who volunteered because they had the least to lose. (We kept remembering what happened to the organizers of the 1970 strikes.) At first a committee of about 10 people was set up. On Monday we elected representatives from each department to the strike committee, and the committee increased to about 40 people. We started organizing essential services within the shipyards. Some machinery in the shipyards must be continually maintained. We organized a team to prevent damage to shipyard property. We also kept a patrol around the walls of the yard because we were afraid of provocation.

Later on we organized entertainment, with performers from the Baltic Opera and Coastal Theatre. It followed the Mass, which was at 5pm. We also showed films hired from the local film library. Before the film we listened to the news. Some of the workers who had free time played cards.

How are the new unions being organized?

The Strike Committee became the founding committee of the new union. A presidium of nine members was set up. This will be a temporary presidium until we have had elections (in accordance with the statute of the NSZZ Solidarity). Representatives of the committee meet regularly with the directors to discuss pay and other matters. The directors are usually co-operative. It was different just after the strike ended, when we were relinquishing control of shipyard property to the bosses. Then the bosses wanted to re-establish their lost power. We protested to Jagielski and they calmed down.

About 85% of the employees joined the new unions. We expect that this percentage will increase. Those who did not join either stayed with the old union, that is the Metalworkers' Union, or simply don't want to be in any union. People with senior positions in the shipyards are probably against joining the new union because, according to its statute, they cannot hold office.

What were the old unions like?

The officials of the old unions were not elected democratically. When they completed their terms they themselves nominated most of the new candidates. Only a small percentage could be nominated from the floor, during the elections. (For example, for 10 nominated by the old committee only one or two were nominated from the floor.) It was decided in advance who would be on the new committee. There were cases of rigged elections. Newly-elected committees would proceed to a hired bar to settle the details over a drink. To be a union activist was a career. The old unions had an extremely limited range of activity. In the shipyard the metalworkers' union was popularly known as the Travel Agency because its main task was booking workers' holidays and refunding travel costs. It also dealt with the distribution of produce such as potatoes and onions. These unions, however, did not fulfil their basic role of defending the rights of the workers.

I was sacked from my previous job with the agreement of the union, and the guy who signed that agreement didn't even bother to talk to me.

In what way did the old unions deal with matters of safety and hygiene at work, and what do the new unions plan to do about them?

These matters were totally neglected by the old unions. Bosses ordered the workers to do jobs that could damage their health: in theory it was possible to refuse but in practice there was always someone else willing to do the job, and besides the bosses would take revenge. Wage supplements for people working under bad conditions are low, considering the damage their health suffers. Sometimes these supplements aren't paid to the workers at all under various pretexts. Safety equipment is inadequate and limited. If it is too expensive they don't buy it. To install a ventilator to protect workers from lung diseases costs 100,000 zlotys — absurdly, the management prefers to pay compensation to installing a ventilator.

The new unions intend to deal with these matters: this is in the new statute. A candidate for a trade union post will have to present his/her programme of action. If he is elected and he doesn't keep his promises he could be kicked out even before the next elections. It's important for all employees to monitor officials. An essential function of the new unions is to protect workers, not only in matters of health and safety but in **all** matters. After the 1970 strike the leaders were persecuted. The second point of the Gdansk agreement guarantees that the leaders will not be persecuted this time. The new unions must ensure that this agreement is kept.

In the two years before the strikes, the underground paper Robotnik (The Worker) was published. Did this paper influence the initial strike action and the course which the strike took?

Neither of us were activists before the strike. We were ordinary workers. **Robotnik** reached us only from time to time, not regularly. We used to read it and pass it on to people we trusted: so every copy had many readers. This is an individual matter; the paper did not influence **us** much. Several major things influenced us: a lot of people listen to Western radio in Polish (BBC V.O.A.); the official press irritated us: our experiences in 1970; and the personal influence of the strikers of 1970 such as Kolodziej, Gwiazda, Walesa, Walentynowicz. (When I pointed out to the interviewees that these were the editors of **Robotnik** they agreed amidst laughter.) These last two points were of great importance for the course of the strike.

We knew that to go outside the shipyard gates would be dangerous and that we had to protect the shipyard from damage. We also had to maintain order in the shipyard. We were completely successful in these things. In some matters our organization improved on that before the strike: for example, we succeeded in distributing cold drinks to the workers which had proved impossible before the strike. The P.A. system worked better during the strike than it does now.

During the strike consumption of alcohol in the shipyard was forbidden. At the beginning of the strike a foreman was thrown out for drunkenness. Before being thrown out he was paraded around the shipyard in a cart; it was a short of symbolic pillory.

Will your own union paper be important in the future?

Yes, the shipyards, like other large works, publish their own information bulletins. It is important that we have complete information and that workers' resolutions be published in full. The omission of even one sentence can change the entire meaning.

Are you optimistic or pessimistic about the future? Do you think that the free unions will be disbanded in the future or will they become a permanent factor in Polish society?

We are guarded optimists. There may be difficulties: this depends on external and internal conditions, which are liable to change. It's important to observe the Gdansk agreement and the new union statute.

This is our last chance to democratize our country. We must use the strength we have to organize and maintain the free unions. If we fail it will be tragic.

INTERVIEW WITH MKS PRESIDIUM MEMBER —By Michael Siegert

(*The following is an interview conducted by* Michael Siegert *with Josef Pryhiliski, a 37-year-old welder at the Budimor shipyard equipment factory. He was then a member of the 16-strong Presidium of the Inter-factory Strike Committee of Gdansk-Gdynia-Sopot.*)

How did the strike begin at your workplace?

On Thursday 14 August we heard that the Lenin Shipyard was on strike. I then began organizing. Several of us spoke to the workforce and on the 15th we went on strike too.

What were your motives?

Our standard of living had worsened. We cannot manage without the strike. Things are getting so bad that we'll have to work a 12-or 15-hour day in 3, 4 or 5 years.

Did you have personal reasons?

I'd already been to the trade union about a flat. As soon as I entered they asked me, 'What are your beliefs, comrade?' As if I had to be a Party member or should have applied to join. In the end I got tired of waiting, got building permission and built it myself, 44 square meters. I have now been waiting 8 years for permission to move in.

Why does nothing work in this system?

From the smallest workshop to the biggest factory in Poland there is nobody who has any responsibility.

How can such responsibility be achieved?

Through free trade unions.

In the West trade unions restrict themselves to wages and social questions. Should they do more?

I believe that we in Poland will get involved in production after the creation of free trade unions. Many of us have ideas. Only the workers know what is good for production.

For example?

The factories are given the task by the government of producing as much as possible. There are, for example, many black and white TVs in storage which cannot be disposed of. Too many have been produced.

How can the control of production be organized?

Each factory elects delegates who supervise production and the market. They go into the shops to see what people want. There are all these propaganda words: everything quicker, better and cheaper. But one cannot produce faster just like that; the quality of the product declines.

Aren't these questions political?

Yes. Our representatives will even sit in the Sejm like the representatives of the official unions. (Reporter's note: Another Presidium member, Andrej Gwiazda, replied to this question, 'There are still four years to go before the next elections'.)

Won't you come into conflict with the Party if you, for example, put social expenditures before arms?

We pay 50 to 60 zlotys a month to the union. I think the first thing will be to spend this money properly.

Do you think capitalism will return to Poland?

Party members have a lot of privileges, such as homes and money. They live well. A real Communist is poor. They are not real communists.

Is it better for a worker to work in a state-owned or private factory?

My personal view is that it is not important for a good worker where he works. Here in Poland he is better off if he's lazy. An idler gets the same pay as someone who works hard. Under capitalism he would be thrown out: people say—good work, good wages.

Do you send delegates to other factories to urge them to strike?

The Committee does not urge others to strike, but many people come to us and tell us they support us.

V THE FARMERS BACK THE WORKERS

PROCLAMATION TO THE STRIKING WORKERS

In Solidarnosc No.7 various unofficial peasant organisations expressed their support for the workers struggle and at the same time called for aid for agriculture. Below we print further statements by independent peasant organisations.

In Poland agriculture is largely in the hands of small, private peasant farmers. Most of these farmers are poor in comparison with the living standards of skilled workers in the cities and at the same time many workers retain some link with agriculture. The regime has tended to favour the richer farmers while hitting the poorer peasants in various ways. One such measure — a new peasant pension law which was in reality a new tax burden for the less well off peasants — produced widespread opposition and the re-birth of independent peasant activist groups in various parts of the country.

The following documents come from these new groups of activists, but they reflect the widespread peasant sympathy for the workers' struggles. The first document is in fact a summary made available to us by the UK-based Information Centre for Polish Affairs.

THE PEASANT SELF-DEFENCE COMMITTEE OF THE GROJEC COUNTY

Zbrosza Duza, 24th August 1980

A PROCLAMATION TO THE WORKERS STRIKING ON THE BALTIC COAST (SUMMARY)

Brother workers,

Following the appeals by the state and party authorities, urging the people to carry out a national debate on the bad state of affairs in the Polish Republic, we, the peasants from a number of villages in Radom province gathered on Sunday, 24th August, in Zbrosza Duza, to discuss in a public spirit the fate of our country. We considered whether the demands, which you are putting forward by means of your strike, are just. We decided that they are just and worthy of our support. Your rightful struggle for trade unions, independent from the party and state apparatus, aids our own attempts to establish a similar trade union organization for agricultural workers. With this aim in mind we have already established in several parts of the country the Peasants' Self-Defence Committees and the Farmers' Trade Union. We assure you that despite the harassment and obstacles created by the official authorities we shall continue our activity. We understand that these actions are necessary to bring changes leading to an agricultural policy which will ensure that there is

v

enough of our own Polish bread for everybody and we do not have to humiliate ourselves by begging abroad for credits to buy grain. We join your struggle to put an end to repressions and arrests and together with you we call for the release of political prisoners, amongst whom there are also peasants, like Jan Kozlowski, a farmer from Tarnobrzeg province, imprisoned because he had expressed his concern at the state of the nation. We insist that the authorities accept your demands without delay, for delay is damaging to the country, and make it possible for you to go back to work. Whoever can deny the righteousness of your demand for family allowances to be raised to the level paid to the police nd the security service? The Polish media keep silent about your demands out of fear that the whole Polish nation is ready to support them. We want to tell you, brother workers, that the state and party dignitaries, who demand sacrifices from you, in the name of the common welfare, do not set an example themselves. They pay themselves high salaries, yet want to economize on the money paid to the workers. They have passed a government bill granting privileges to the families of the party and state dignitaries, even to the third generation. Because of his family position, even a grandson of a high ranking official may collect a state pension, equivalent to 75% of that dignitary's salary. Let it be known to you, brother workers, that the authorities who take such care of their own families forget about the families of the peasants. Only peasants' families are deprived of any allowances. We are concerned that in their latest speeches neither the First Secretary of the Party nor the Prime Minister announced any changes in the present disastrous agricultural policy, which has resulted in poor food supplies in the whole country. You must know that in recent years an official government bill was passed which changed the status of the rightful owners of farm holdings to that of the temporary occupiers. In order to pass on your own farm to your son or daughter, you have to have permission from a head of a local administrative council and heads of local councils rule according to their own wishes. The education system in the villages is also a blow against peasant families. The farmers are deprived of all rights to defend themselves against the misuse of power. The publicly advertised bill concerning the so-called benefits of the farmers' pension scheme, in practice should be called a bill on the methods of destruction of family farming. The only sensible way to run Polish agriculture is to support family farming. We hope, brother workers, that you win the fullest possible concessions. We declare our solidarity with you. We present you with 12,312 zloties which we have collected on your behalf. At the same time we inform you that we gather and shall continue to gather in Zbrosza Duza on each Sunday after High Mass and we invite everybody to take part in these meetings in order to consider how to resolve the country's difficulties resulting from the present official policy.

AGRICULTURAL DEMANDS

(Demands submitted by the 17 village councils of Stegna and ratified at a general meeting of delegates on 24 August 1980, in Drewnicy by 980 householders.)

1. An increase in the amount of coal available. Abolition of allocation of coal and coke as well as speculation in coal.
2. Abolition of allocation and limits on the purchase of agricultural machinery. Machinery should be made available on the market at the same prices as they are to state farms.
3. A decrease in the price of fertilizer and insecticides of at least 40% and both should be made available to the G.S. storehouses.
4. Guarantee of an adequate amount of the necessary fodder for farmers, of an adequate quality.
5. A refund on gas used by farmers with their own tractors based on the amount of arable as a compensation for the rise in oil prices — 50% minimum.
6. Abolition of allocations and limits on building materials and an adequate supply of these items for farming villages.
7. Allowing farmers to buy land from state farms if it neighbours their own land.
8. The formation of agricultural trade unions to protect farmers' rights.
9. Lower the retirement age of women to 50 and men to 55, and lower the pension contributions by 50%.
10. To permit the closest relatives of a farmer to inherit his savings if he dies, without any legal complications.
11. To increase the amount of financial assistance to handicapped persons in rural families.
12. To activate rural medical services. There is a shortage of staff at existing clinics.
13. We demand categorically an elimination of nepotism and bribery in state agencies and co-operatives.
14. We demand that it be made possible to teach religion at school.
15. To increase the availability of foodstuffs in the village: of meat and meat products, sugar and its products as well as sugar for bees, baked goods, chemicals and hardware and tools.
16. An increase of 100% in the purchase price of grain and seeds so as to guarantee profitable production.
17. An increase of at least 50% of the cost of production in the purchase price of milk and foodstuffs.
18. The construction of an irrigation system which would reach eachfarm (especially in Ziclawy).
19. The possibility for farmers to choose to contract agricultural products (to the state).
20. A decrease of 50% in the amount charged to farmers for the use of combines and harvesters.
21. We demand the establishment of separate flood ordinances for the Zulawy area. Zulawy is in a depressed area where the heavy soil holds water. The farmers suffer huge losses because of this, more so than elsewhere.
22. We demand that state prices be taken as the basis for the calculation of compensation for losses, that is the state prices prevailing at the time the declaration of loss is made.
23. Reform of insurance articles prejudicial to the interests of farmers.
24. The implementation of decisions made to build side roads.

vi BUILDING SOLIDARITY

It is far too early and information is too incomplete to paint an adequate picture of the building of the new trade union, Solidarity. But we publish below a few documents indicating some of the thinking of the worker activists.

First, there is a short appeal by the Founding Committee of the Independent, Self-Managed Trade Union to the Lenin Shipyard workers in Gdansk on 5 September, within a week of the end of the strike. The text shows the sober, cautious and practical attitude of the workers' leaders in the wake of their great victory.

Second, there is an example of the approach taken to setting up a new union, in this case drawn from Lublin. The document is a resolution establishing the local Founding Committee of a new trade union centre.

Thirdly, there is the communiqué after the first national meeting of delegates that gathered in Gdansk on 17 September to start discussing the shape of the new union.

Fourthly, we publish the draft programme of activities of the new union as put forward by the founding committee for discussion among the Gdansk shipyard workers.

In the face of the authorities' harassment of the new union, the leaders of Solidarity decided to call a national protest strike. We publish a statement from Solidarity's Warsaw leadership (known as the Mazowsze Committee after the general region in which Warsaw is situated) explaining why the protest strike is being called. We also publish a statement by the national leadership of Solidarity of 1 October affirming the strike call.

The October 3rd strike showed the country that Solidarity had firmly established itself as the organised leadership of the Polish workers. Yet it had still not been given access to the mass media nor had it been granted legal recognition. We print a resolution of 6 October outlining Solidarity's demands for access to the media.

Finally, in response to the attacks and slanders from other East European countries, a short but impressive and revealing resolution from the workers of the huge Nowa Huta Lenin Steel Works shows what a formidable weight lies behind the new union.

FOUNDING COMMITTEE APPEAL

5 September 1980

Thanks to solidarity and prudence, the recent strike has finished with an agreement with the Government Commission. In the same spirit of prudence and solidarity we will undertake the realization of the conditions of the agreement, especially its most important articles which we consider to be:

1. An active part in the creation of the trade union statute and in the preparation of union elections. Very soon the draft statute, which has been prepared by legal experts, will become available. Regardless of the fact that a group of specialists at the MKS will examine the draft, we appeal (to everyone) to send their comments and proposals to us concerning our statute.

2. The supervision of the implementation of the accords of the agreement with the government commission in matters concerning our enterprise. Specifically what we have in mind here is a correct procedure being carried out in preparation for the elections to our trade unions, and the supervision of contributions to the enterprise's social fund. At the same time the Founding Committee will work with the directorate of the shipyard to implement the temporary agreement on pay rises for all employees. This also involves dealing with matters which require immediate attention.

This is something which all those who wished to join the Independent Self-Managed Trade Union must take part in, and not only those who decided to represent their factory during the strike and presently make up the Founding Committee. We can only count on ourselves and on people of good will who can help us in specialist matters. In accord with the basic principles of our state we are the co-owners of our places of work and the trade union formed by us will guarantee the realization of this right.

As co-owners we have the moral right and duty to concern ourselves with the wellbeing of our enterprise and its products. The Founding Committee of the Independent Self-Managed Trade Union appeals to shipyard workers to stand firm on production demands and the shipyard director's appeal.

We are repeating our strike motto 'Prudence and Solidarity' during this difficult time of forming the trade union and of catching-up on the lost production of the shipyard.

In August the eyes of the world were upon us, and our countrymen placed all their hopes in us. We are obliged to a common sense of responsibility and productive activity to our enterprise.

Appeal of the Founding Committee of the Independent, Self-Managed Trade Union at the Lenin Shipyard in Gdansk

LUBLIN FOUNDING COMMITTEE APPEAL

Acting in accordance with the principles contained in the text of the agreement signed in the Gdansk shipyard on 31 August and recognising the leading role of the Party and the Socialist Order of the State, the Founding Committees of Independent Self-Managed Trade Unions from enterprises in the East-Central region have decided to set up, starting on 10 September, an East-Central Inter-factory Founding Committee of the Independent Self-Managed Trade Unions based in Lublin.

A committee has been formed, whose members are: Stanislaw Daniel - FSC (lorry plant), Lublin; Czeslaw Niezgoda - Locomotive works, Lublin; Ryszard Kuc - WSK (transport equipment factory), Swidnik; Jerzy Gregorowicz - ZWN Unitra (electrical appliances), Lubarczow; Aleksander Chrzanowski - Argomet, Lublin; Zdzislaw Kudyk — _azoty (fertiliser plant), Pulawy; Jan Nakonieczny - INS (Fertiliser research institute), Pulawy; Boleslaw Cwikla - Transport Communications Enterprise No.6, Lublin; Jan Bochra - the Lublin car repair works, Lublin; Wieslaw Krzyszczak - the Lublin Pharmaceutical Works, Lublin; Ryszard Jankowski - The Enterprise for the Conservation of Historical Buildings, Lublin.

The elected representatives of the Founding Committees of the Independent Self-Governing Trade Unions from enterprises in the East-Central region, the list of whose names is contained in an addendum to this resolution, elected—with one abstention—the Committee Presidium, whose members are: Chairman - Czeslaw Neizgoda (Locomotive Works, Lublin); Vice-chairman - Stanislaw Daniel (Heavy Vehicle Factory, Lublin); Vice-chairman - Ryszard Kuc (WSK, Swidnik). The elected representatives unanimously agreed that the attached list of enterprises represented at the opening meeting of the Committee will be supplemented by those enterprises that make a request to join. At the same time the representatives passed a unanimous resolution, stating that the Committee remains open to the representatives of those work-places or groups of employees who will be elected democratically and without the application of any constraints on the wishes of the electors.

The Committee, basing itself on the contents of the agreements signed in Gdansk on 31 August, reserves the right to obtain permission from the provincial authorities in Lublin for the publication in the local media of the text of the following resolution within a fixed period of time, as well as undertaking on the part of the provincial governor of Lublin, the local authorities and the management of local enterprises, to ensure appropriate conditions for the establishment and subsequent activity of independent, self-governing trade unions.

The Committee appeals to all enterprises and groups of employees in the East-Central region and to all individual employees to increase productive effort in every workshop and at every post. The elected representatives of the aforementioned enterprises demand that the provincial authorities make available to the Committee an appropriate office in Lublin, without delay, as well as all essential means to conduct its business in a normal way. The Committee reserves the right to avail itself of specialist advice and to set up local advisory centres. In the event of the provincial authorities not fulfilling the duties incumbent upon them on the strength of the agreement signed in Gdansk, the Committee reserves the right to take a decision on the declaration of a strike by the enterprises and groups of employees that it represents. The Committee will cease to function following elections to independent, self-governing trade unions. The elected representatives unanimously empowered the Committee to sign this resolution and to represent the independent, self-governing trade unions in all matters relating to their organisation and activity.

This resolution is signed on behalf of the elected representatives by: (12 signatures follow, for names see above)

We respectfully request the provincial governor to legalise this resolution on 11 September 1980.

East-Central Inter-factory Founding Committee of the Independent Self-Governing Trade Unions based in Lublin.

(The provincial governor, Mieczyslaw Stepien, wrote on the bottom of the text: 'Received: 11.9.80.')

STATEMENT FROM NATIONAL DELEGATE MEETING

On 17 September 1980, at the headquarters of the Inter-factory Founding Committee of the Independent Self-Managed Trade Unions (NSZZ) in Gdansk, delegates from others areas of Poland assembled. At this meeting a review of the state of the NSZZ in various towns and regions of the country was carried out. Participants in the discussion were representatives from the Founding Committees of the NSZZ in Szczecin, Krakow, Katowice Steel Works, Mazowsze, Bydgoszcz, Walbrzych, Krosno, Elblag, Lodz, Prudnik, Jastrzebie Zdroj, Stalowa Wola, Wroclaw, Andrychow, Lublin, Bytom, Opole, Siemianowice, Toryn, Tychy, Plock, Kolobrzeg, Poznan, Slupsk, Gorzow Wielkopolski, Rzeszow, Zywiec, Kozle, and Gdansk and also a representative of the NSZZ of Scientific, Technical and Educational Workers in Krakow.

The review of organisational matters revealed that at the present moment over 3 million people from about 3½ thousand factories had joined or expressed the wish to join the NSZZ. The situation varies considerably and is dependent on the strength of workers' solidarity, the attitude of the local authorities and the sizes of the workplaces. While noting the progress being made in the foundation and organisational work of the independent autonomous unions, it was revealed that it is taking place in difficult conditions and must wrestle constantly with obstacles. In workplaces where a majority are female, the activities of the NSZZ are hampered by a policy of discrimination and by the pressure of the economic administration. In weaker or less numerous centres the emergence of the new unions is accompanied by fear of victimisation and reprisals. Several actions of the authorities such as detention and interrogation by the security forces of workers' delegates, or burdening them with police surveillance, create a source of new tensions. In most regions access to the mass media for the independent trade unions remains closed, and in certain areas there is evidence of disinformation techniques. The old unions from the CRZZ (Central Trade Union Council) try to conduct a propaganda full of lies about alleged losses suffered by workers crossing over to join our unions. Local and regional authorities in many parts of the country do not carry into effect the spirit of the August agreements. Our unions grapple with local difficulties, while the management of many companies create continuous obstacles to the activities of the NSZZ.

Independent Self-Managed Trade Unions have been formed throughout the whole country, also in many cities and regions which were not represented at the conference. Representatives of the NSZZ at the Gdansk conference stated that the establishment of new trade unions expresses the aims of the broad mass of working people of the whole country to possess independent and authentic representation. Concern was expressed that achieving conditions of the Agreement (concerning the creation of new unions and guaranteeing no discrimination against them), was being met, already at this inception stage, by many basic difficulties. Note was taken, at this meeting, of the resolution by the Council of State on 13 September which outlined the temporary principles of registration. Representatives of the NSZZ, while expressing uneasiness with certain sections of that resolution, stressed with considerable vigour that an efficient and speedy carrying out of that registration by the appointed channels was in the public interest.

The position of the NSZZ vis-à-vis the present state of the union, and concerning registration was outlined in special declarations. The conference recognised that further activities of the NSZZ in the spirit of solidarity and caution require broad understanding and coordination. With this aim in mind, a Provisional Liaison

Commission of the NSZZ was set up. The proposal of the Gdansk NSZZ that the seat of the Commission be in Gdansk was accepted. During the first meeting of the Commission Lech Walesa was elected Chairman of the Commission. It will be the task of the Commission to organise common action for the NSZZ at national level and to ensure the participation of the NSZZ in work on new legislation on trade unions, labour law, social and economic policies and consultation and coordination in controlling the fruition of the agreements between workers and the government, as well as to conduct interventions. It will also be one of the tasks of the Liaison Commission to outline the methods of actions in the context of a homogeneous single union. The Liaison Commission will carry out the formalities of registering that union, which will encompass the Inter-Factory Founding Committees, and whose region of operation is the entire country.

DRAFT PROGRAMME OF CURRENT ACTION

The Independent Trade Union represents the interests of the workers in it, and in their name it negotiates with employers as well as with the administration and the state. The activities we propose to undertake are premised on the firm belief that the prosperity of the Fatherland, the entire society and every inhabitant is dependent upon the effective defence of the rights of all employees and a genuine representation of the interests of individual specialized groups,

Our Union will demand that individual workers and their groups have a real possibility to come forth with initiatives and that these be examined seriously by the management, and if necessary by their superiors. The absolutely necessary condition for the realization of such a demand is a frank openness in social and economic affairs. The Independent Trade Union, however, has no intention of interfering with affairs under the competence of the management nor to replace it, nor to be responsible for its activities.

Presently the Independent Trade Union is concerned with:
— overseeing the implementation of the protocols of the agreement worked out between the government and the MKS on 31 August 1980
— organizing its activities
— resolving the most pressing problems
In accord with Article 9 of the protocol of 31 August 1980 agreed by the Government of the Polish People's Republic and the MKS, which deals with the means of compensation for price rises which will be worked out by the end of 1980, the Union proposes that the compensation be based on the following:

— make allowances for price rises in workers' wages as well as in pensions
— pay these above-mentioned allowances into family allowances (in the case of single persons, as a separate social fund).

The basis upon which the allowance should be calculated is the social minimum, that is, the amount necessary for subsistence for one person for one month. The present minimum is 2200 zlotys. In the future independent research institutions should determine how much this minimum is. This allowance should be awarded according to the number of people in the family of the worker or pensioner, as the increase in the amount spent on basic necessities is greater than the number of people in the family.

If, for example, costs rise 10%, then the allowance for one person would be 220 zlotys, for a family of 5 — 1100 zlotys, and for a family of 2 — 440 zlotys.

This allowance should be introduced no later than 2 January 1981. This is a matter of such importance, that Article 10 of the agreement seeks to regulate meat prices to an average, by lowering commercial store prices and raising normal prices. If price rises go beyond the allowances system authorised here, those who will suffer the most will be the lower-paid workers and pensioners. They should also receive some sort of compensation in case this happens.

2. The most fundamental tool in the struggle for the rights of the workers are collective work agreements. We must try to ensure that the Independent Trade Unions are part of these agreements alongside other unions.

To achieve this the laws dealing with the following must be changed:
— abolition of the monopoly held by central authorities concerning craft unions when collective agreements are reached
— abolition of the need to clear the text of agreements with the Ministry of Labour and Social Affairs.
— abolition of the monopoly of the Ministers of the Central Board of Co-operatives in making agreements on behalf of the employers.
— abolition of the extreme limitations on the parties in government pay agreements on the basis of Article 79. The new collective agreements concluded by the Union should have a temporary character with a duration of no longer than three years. Furthermore there should be a possibility of giving three months' notice (for agreements longer than a year).

Agreements concluded by the Independent Trade Union can have either a business or professional character, as according to the envisaged statute, only the representatives of the enterprise which the agreement will concern will take part in drawing up the agreement. In the immediate future the main purpose which the conclusion of such agreements should serve is the rationalization of the system of wages by a limitation of the number of pay grades.

These should consist of a basic wage, a supplement and a premium, which should not be more than a specific percentage of the basic wage. All other payments must be abolished such as the so-called 'recognition premium' and other kinds of remuneration paid at the discretion of the enterprise. The agreement concluded by the Independent Trade Union must also become the means for limiting the piece-work system, which should be totally abolished in due course. For the moment it is necessary to radically limit overtime but without limiting the pay.

3. At the outbreak of the strike the majority of enterprises dissolved their enterprise councils, and gave the impression that they did not represent the employees, but the superior institutions, among these the CRZZ. Because of this new enterprise councils must be elected as soon as possible. According to the agreement made immediately after the war, these should become organs of the enterprise, independent of the trade unions and not tied to any superior organs.

Every employee has an absolute right to vote for enterprise councils and the elections should be carried out according to a proportional system. This means that every union organisation as well as every other organisation at the enterprise would have the right to present its candidates. Voters would vote for a given list.The council would be made up according to the number of votes on each list. Thus if three lists are proposed: NSZZ, official trade unions (CRZZ), and a third list put forward by a group of workers, and the first list gets 60% of the votes and the other two 20% each, then 60% of the representatives on the enterprise council will be from the NSZZ, 20% from the official trade unions, and 20% would represent the other list.

Alongside the enterprise councils local branches of the various trade unions will also be active in the enterprise and they will influence the activities of the council only via their representatives.

3.1. The enterprise councils will deal with issues concerning the social fund (vacations, children's summer camps), housing, supervision of the benefits and loans fund, as well as other activities listed in the labour laws.

This will also involve participation in decision-making in cases reviewing employees' complaints about administrative penalties, participation in consultations on the drawing up of work regulations, determining together with the plant management the division of labour time in enterprises where this is not stipulated by regulations, being consulted about holiday plans, etc.

3.2. It is the responsibility of the enterprise council to defend the employees' interests as far as it can. If the council fails to fulfil its obligations they will be taken up by the independent trade union. This relates in particular to finding out whether people are being penalized for taking part in union activity. If they are, then the independent trade union is duty-bound to call a strike, if all other means of solving the problem have been exhausted.

4. In order to guarantee the safety of the workers on the job, our Union will examine new jobs as well as periodically examine existing positions to ensure that they meet the necessary safety and health standards. The conclusions of these examinations will be submitted to the management and the enterprise council. In instances where a job threatens the workers' health or life, the Unions is obliged to forbid its members to work there. In cases where a worker, in conformity with the demands of the union, refuses to work, the appropriate interpretation of the strike clause will be applied.

We will attempt to enforce the laws concerning occupational diseases, and will attempt to obtain a definition of 'occupational disease' and 'dangerous and unhealthy conditions' so as to include within the health regulations all those who suffer ill health as a result of their jobs.

5. The Independent Trade Union will attempt to change the labour law so as to return the legal equality between the employer and the employee.

The particular propositions concerning these changes required detailed elaboration. At present we can only mention a few. For example, strengthening of the role of work agreements especially as far as wages are concerned (which was already discussed in the appendix to Point 21 in the Agreement protocol) and also a more precise definition of the kind of work and the place or places where it is to be done.

Hasty changes require changes in the regulations concerning the termination of employment without reason. Regardless of article 2 in the protocol agreement concerning strikes, this involves the introduction of regulations to permit the employee to terminate his employment without notice in the event that the enterprise commits a serious breach of its obligations (this obviously requires detailed formulation in the statutes). The legal equality of the parties is also infringed upon by the regulations on awards and fines, which can give the impression that the employee is subject to the authority of the administration of the enterprise. Awards, in conformity with what we have noted about collective agreements, must be stopped. Fines, meanwhile, should have the character of duly agreed upon monetary penalties of a limited amount. An arbitration committee and judges should adjudicate in this matter.

Changes are also needed in the regulations concerning definitions of pay and work by:
— a specifically granted right for the worker to submit such a statement as well
— a limit on the possibility of transferring an employee to another job without a formal notice (Art. 42, No. 4)

The legal equality between contracting parties is broken by numerous stipulations which make employment at a new place of work conditional upon the manner in which the employee's old job had been terminated. An especially gross infringement of equality which occurs in the activities of arbitration and appeal commissions is the impossibility of obtaining legal representation for the employee, whereas the enterprise as a rule has legal consultants at its disposal.

6. The Independent Trade Union will attempt to lessen the differences in incomes by steadily increasing the wages of the lowest paid. The most important task is to struggle for a system of social security (pensions, family allowances) which will guarantee a social minimum for the family.

We will attempt to bring about a situation in which no mother is forced to take a job because of material need. Point 18 of the protocol concerning the extension of maternity leave refers to this, as does the point concerning price rise supplements.

7. Our union will strive to have the Independent Trade union be given the right to introduce regulations in matters within its field of competence.

8. Very soon we will form a workers' university which will undertake educational activities.

The Inter-factory Founding Committee of the Independent Trade Unions in Gdansk.

Shipyard Workers!

The project of the actual programme given above is presented to you for discussion — to those who have declared themselves willing to join the Independent Trade Union. Also you will formulate the final text of our programme. Through your messangers and your observations and your recommendations on the above programme to the Founding Committee of the Independent Trade Union at the Gdansk shipyard. After being suitably phrased it will be forwarded to the MKZ in Gdansk.

Crowds outside the Lenin Shipyard, Gdansk, 23 August

vii THE OCTOBER 3rd STRIKE

STRIKE CALL EXPLAINED

BY THE WARSAW UNION COMMITTEE

On 29 September 1980 the Integrated Founding Committee of the Independent Self-Managed Trade Unions 'Solidarity' in Gdansk decided to call a nationwide warning and solidarity strike for 3 October. The strike is to start at 12 noon and last until 1 pm. It has been called on the basis of Art.33, statute I, point 1 of the Union's Statute.

The strike has been called for the following reasons: the authorities are not fully implementing the agreements concerning the following points: 1. wages agreements, 2. access by the independent self-managed trade unions to mass media, and 3. non-obstruction of the activities of the independent self-managed trade unions.

The executive of the unions of Mazowsze region decided that the following enterprises are to join the strike: Ursus (Mechanical Works), FSO (car factory), TEWA (Communications equipment), Nowotko, Polcolor (TV sets), MZK (city transport), MPT (taxis). In the above-named enterprises, local union Founding Committees will decide which departments are to strike so as to minimise the damage caused by the stoppages. The striking enterprises will hoist Polish national flags. The strike will start and end with the sounding of sirens. **Only the predetermined departments will take part.** This will prove our strength, our discipline and our organising ability. Those enterprises which do not take part in the strike, but which wish to demonstrate their solidarity with us, are requested to: 1. sound their sirens at noon and at 1 pm., 2. hoist Polish national flags, and 3. demonstrate their solidarity in some other way, as for example posters or the wearing of armbands.

Independent Self-Managed Trade Unions of the Mazowsze Region
Warsaw **30 September 1980**

WHY THE STRIKE IS STILL ON
—By the Gdansk Leadership

On 1 October 1980 a meeting was held in the Gdansk Regional Governor's Office between the Deputy Prime Minister Jagielski and representatives of Party and Government, and the representatives of the 'Solidarity' with its chairman, Lech Walesa. During the meeting, which lasted several hours, problems raised by 'Solidarity' were discussed. The solution of these problems would allow the calling-off of the 1-hour long warning strike which is to take place on 3 October. Representatives of 'Solidarity' attended the meeting hoping that the authorities would suggest specific ideas which would remove the current difficulties concerning the organisation and activities of the Independent Self-Managed Trade Unions, access to the mass media and the consideration of the workers' suggestions concerning the division of sums allocated for wage increases. 'Solidarity' has suggested that agreements concerning wages be implemented not later than 20 October. At first, agreement on these points seemed possible. A working group consisting of the representatives of both sides were set up to consider a joint communique. After an interval, the government's side presented its own draft, which did not contain any specific undertakings. 'Solidarity' representatives stated that in the proposed text the representatives of the government had avoided any binding undertakings on the issues which led to the strike being called.

On receiving the report of its representatives, the executive of 'Solidarity' took the view that its representatives have done their best to convince the government's side of the necessity to remove the reasons for the strike. The executive states once again that it approached the negotiations with an honest intention of reaching agreement. The failure of the negotiations is therefore not its fault. The executive repeats Lech Walesa's statement, that: 'Our union approaches the difficult political situation in the country with proper seriousness and, as we have stated on numerous occasions, wishes to contribute to a solution of the current crisis. This is, however, conditional on the full implementation of the agreements.' Consequently, the strike we have called for does not constitute a departure from the agreements. It is an expression of protest against the creation of conditions which prevent the agreement from being put into practice.

Executive of the Integrated Founding Committee of the Independent Self-Managed Trade Unions in Gdansk, 'Solidarity'
Gdansk **1 October 1980**

(Document made available by the Information Centre for Polish Affairs.)

SOLIDARITY CALLS FOR A DAILY PAPER

To the Deputy Premier
Mieczyslaw Jagielski

According to the agreement of 31 August 1980 between the Government commission and the Inter-factory Strike Committee based in the Gdansk shipyard, and the agreement with the Strike Committee in the Katowice Steelworks, the National Coordinating Committee of Independent Self-Managed Trade Unions 'Solidarity' demands the following:
— an opportunity to publish a national daily of circulation not smaller than that of **Glos Pracy** (official trade union paper), to be increased according to needs, and to publish regional periodicals, books and pamphlets;
— access to mass media: television broadcasts of press conferences of the Union 'Solidarity', not less than once a week for 10 minutes nationwide and 20 minutes on local channels, radio broadcasts not shorter than 45 minutes, regular reporting of 'Solidarity' statements and news by persons authorised by 'Solidarity', a weekly one-hour radio and television programme devoted to the Union movement — prepared by a team formed by 'Solidarity' — and similar programmes on local radio and television.

The Coordinating Committee of 'Solidarity' is convinced that only objective information can secure social peace and conscious well-considered social action.

Coordinating Committee of 'Solidarity'
Gdansk **6 October 1980**

NOWA HUTA SPEAKS FOR SOLIDARITY

We speak on behalf of the 40,000 workers of the Lenin steelworks. During the August strike we supported the coastal shipyard workers. Our strike was organised in support of your demands, the demands of all the working people. The aim of our action was to win for you access to the press, radio and television. The signing of the agreements with the government commission was our first opportunity to see the representatives of the coastal workers. Thank you for your perseverance — without it there would be no 'Solidarity'.

Today our union has over 7 million members. We are the majority of the working people in Poland who believe that socialism is a system of social justice and that it is possible to restore the highest values: truth, justice, recognition for honest work and respect for man. Our activity does not impair the foundations of socialism in our country. We have only condemned those who distorted its basic tenets. Now, when the existence of the 'Solidarity' union is a fact, we are surprised to hear about statements by leaders of the fraternal socialist countries who are anxious to help our nation. It is we who represent the nation! The political authorities and the government have put forward a programme of far-reaching reforms. We would like to see them realised with consistency, and to avoid yet another period of 'renewal'. As working people we can guarantee the realisation of these reforms with our own honest work. All of us have the good of our country at heart.

Steelworkers' Committee of the Lenin Steelworks, Nowa Huta

18 October 1980

viii THE REPRESSION RENEWED

In order to re-launch its drive against the workers, the regime must claim for itself the right to decide who can express their views on the country's problems and who cannot. They will do this by, first, trying to jail one group as 'anti-socialist', then linking it to a second group, and so on until political expression is effectively muzzled. From this it is but a short step to recasting the whole working class upsurge of this year as a conspiracy by the Central Intelligence Agency.

The regime set out on this road during the August crisis by arresting many KOR leaders at the height of the strike — an action against which KOR immediately protested in the first document printed below. But then, in an historic act of working class solidarity, the workers in Gdansk insisted that the KOR leaders must be released as a condition for ending their strike.

In September, however, a former member of a group called the Movement for Human and Citizens' Rights (Polish initials ROPCiO) was arrested and one of the main leaders of KOR, Jacek Kuron, was viciously slandered on TV. (In November other ROPCiO members were also arrested.)

The letter from Kuron is a response to this TV slander, and the second statement from KOR refers to the arrests. The last series of documents refers to the scandal of the Chief Prosecutor's Office provocation, which is described in Oliver MacDonald's article at the start of this issue.

Kuron is a life-long socialist and former Marxist, and a leading left-wing member of the KOR. He is one of the most outspokenly cautious and moderate opponents of the government, urging slow, step-by-step changes, and warning that without such changes there could be a blood-bath. In a cynically doctored tape-recording of Kuron's voice, however, the TV authorities tried to convey the impression that Kuron was hoping for a blood-bath!

Wojciech Ziembinski and Leszek Moczulski are not socialists (though Socialists in the West will be able to assess their views accurately only when Stalinist censorship is permanently scrapped in Poland). They are fervent nationalists who have been very active in the revival of political life in Poland during the last few years. As we go to press they remain in prison.

STATEMENT AND APPEAL
Social Self-Defense Committee 'KOR'
Warsaw 25 August 1980

The strike movement taking place all over Poland, but primarily on the Baltic, is protracted mainly because the authorities stubbornly refused to negotiate with the Integrated Strike Committees of the Baltic towns. This movement led to far-reaching changes in the composition of the government and the highest echelons of the Polish United Workers' Party. The newly reshuffled authorities have begun the new era of their leadership by continuing to repress the activists of the democratic opposition. Jan Litynski, member of the KSS-'KOR' and editor of **Robotnik** was arrested a week ago. The following lost their freedom 5 days ago: Jan Cywinski, an activist of the Students' Solidarity Committee in Warsaw; Ludwik Dorn, editor of **The Voice**; Urszula Doroszewska, editor of **The Voice**; Sergiusz Kowalski, supporter of the KSS-'KOR'; Dariusz Kupiecki, editor of **Robotnik**; Jacek Kuron, member of the KSS-'KOR' and editor of **Krytyka**; Witold Luczywo, editor of **Robotnik**; Adam Michnik, member of the KSS-'KOR' and editor of **Krytyka**, who is also one of the leading figures of the Independent Publishing Workshop NOWA; Zbigniew Romaszewski, member of the KSS-'KOR' and manager of its Intervention Bureau. Four days ago the following were arrested: Miroslaw Chojecki, member of the KSS-'KOR' and manager of NOWA; Wieslaw Piotr Kecik, member of the KSS-'KOR' and editor of **Placowka**. Three days ago Andrzej Bulc, editor of the Baltic **Robotnik** was detained. We suspect that this is not a complete list. However, due to our telephones being disconnected, our telephone conversations being interrupted and other, similar things we find it difficult to collect information.

The principal reason for these arrests is the persistent work by the KSS-'KOR' undertaken with a view to break through the officially imposed blockade of strike information, information concerning strikes and workers' demands. The law in force in Poland does not allow a person to be detained for more than 48 hours without beingcharged — and even then only under certain conditions, which, however, are not adhered to as a rule.

We strongly protest against this lawlessness. We demand the immediate release of those detained. We appeal to all the members of the public to support this demand. We appeal first of all to the strike committees: demand the immediate release of all the detained activists of the democratic opposition. They acted in the interests and for the benefit of the strikers. We also demand the release of imprisoned activists of the democratic opposition: Jan Kozlowski, Marek Kozlowski and Edmund Zadrozynski and also Tadeusz Kolano. All of them were unjustly sentenced to imprisonment on the basis of false criminal charges. We also ask you to remember the brothers Kowalczyk from Opole, sentenced some 10 years ago to 25 years' imprisonment. They were sentenced on a criminal charge, namely for destroying — with the use of explosives — a lecture hall of the Opole Higher Teachers' School on the eve of a meeting in the honour of police and Security Service officers. However, the method employed by them precluded, in our opinion, any possibility of loss of life or limb. We maintain that they have suffered enough during their 10 years' long imprisonment.

It is impossible to trust the new direction of the government's policy as long as there are political prisoners, the repression continues and lawlessness rules in Poland.

OPEN LETTER TO SHIPYARD WORKERS AND ALL COASTAL WORKERS

By Jacek Kuron

I am turning to you because it is mainly thanks to you that I and my colleagues in the Social Self-Defence Committee 'KOR' were released from prison on 1 September. Our release was one of the demands of the Gdansk agreement. I am writing to you, for today the whole propaganda machinery of the Polish People's Republic is turned against me and 'KOR' with the aim of destroying your achievement: trade unions. The authorities were forced to agree to independent and self-governing trade unions but there are still some who hope they will be able to deprive the trade unions of this independence. The unions are strong thanks to your courage and solidarity, thanks to the genuine activists chosen, controlled and supported by you. The campaign of slander is directed against your courage and its instigators want you to abandon your leaders one by one. On the surface, it concerns Kuron, but soon it may concern Anna Walentynowicz, Lech Walesa, Andrzej Gwiazda, Anna Duda-Gwiazda, Andrzej Kolodziej, Alina Pienkowska, Jacech Pilichowski who — as the statement of the Coordination Committee of Solidarnosc of 24 September 1980 points out — were defended by the 'KOR' when dismissed from work and imprisoned for their struggle for independent trade unions. At first sight it concerns Kuron, but in fact the authorities want you to accept that they can decide who has and who has not the right to be active in trade unions. And then they will choose union leaders acceptable to themselves. There are still people who believe that they can imitate Goebbels: to lie and lie again until the lies stick.

I have the honour to be a member of the 'KOR' which, from the 1st of July, i.e. when the strikes began, has appealed to workers to organise themselves peacefully and appealed to the authorities not to cause a national tragedy but to talk with the democratically elected workers' representatives. Polish television maintains that in an interview given to the Swedish television I incited workers to set fire to party committees. In fact in July and August, warning the authorities against using force against the strikers, I reminded them of the party committees set on fire in December 1970 and June 1976. At the same time I repeated: 'Do not burn down party committees — set up your own instead.' It is strange that Polish television should make me responsible for the blood of coastal workers. But the miracles of television technology will not help them put the blame for the December 1970 massacre and 1976 tortures on me or 'KOR'. We all know well now that we: workers, intellectuals, farmers, are responsible for our country, not party secretaries and ministers. And you, workers at the Coast, and the Silesian miners who support you, the Ursus metal workers, the writers and scholars of Warsaw — demanded the rights and institutions which would enable Poland to develop in peace and freedom. And those who make an outcry about the amount of money your strike cost, have themselves squandered billions of dollars of foreign credits. It is they who are responsible for the present situation and for the lack of opportunity for real improvements within the next few years. We have to face them calmly, even if they should again try to provoke unrest.

On 23 September 1976 with over a dozen people we formed the Workers' Defence Committee. We were ashamed that the intelligentsia had been silent in 1970 and '71, and we wanted to restore its good name. After the brutal suppression of workers' strikes and demonstrations, thousands of workers all over Poland found themselves without jobs. Police custodies were full. Trials began in Warsaw (Ursus) and Radom. Thousands of workers were brutally beaten and tortured. 'KOR' set itself the aim of organizing financial help for people dismissed from work and the families of the imprisoned, to offer legal and—when necessary—medical help, to fight for freedom for the imprisoned and jobs for the sacked. The Workers' Defence Committee appealed to all Poles here and abroad for moral and financial support and therefore from the very start received large sums of money, since people both at home and abroad responded generously to the appeal.

The emergence of 'KOR' activated wide sections of the nation. About a thousand families persecuted in 1976 received help. For this hard work was needed from hundreds of people collecting information about repressions and the means to help the persecuted, establishing contacts, etc. In the action of collecting signatures in defence of the imprisoned thousands of people were not afraid to sign. Among them were both scientists and artists, teachers and representatives of other professions as well as workers and farmers, Security forces have not been able to contain the growing social movement, despite beatings, sometimes severe, despite arrests and sackings, threats and slanders.

After the murder by 'persons unknown' of the 'KOR' collaborator in Krakow, the student Stanislaw Pyjas, and protest demonstrations in Krakow, eleven members and collaborators of 'KOR' were arrested. A mass protest action led not only to their release, but also to the release of workers sentenced to up to nine years' imprisonment. From that time on the opposition movement has been spreading: student solidarity committees and farmers' self-defence committees emerged, as well as founding committees of free trade unions. (In the coastal region among the founders were: Lech Walesa, Anna Walentynowicz, Alina Pienkowska, Andrzej Gwiazda, Andrzej Kolodziej, Anna Duda-Gwiazda, Bogdan Borusewicz and other later leaders of the August 1980 strikes.) Many opposition groups and periodicals have emerged, among them **Robotnik** (The Worker), well-known to workers all over Poland (about one million copies reached their readers), edited collectively by intellectuals and workers; **Placowka** (An Outpost) for farmers and others. In September 1977 'KOR' was transformed into the Social Self-Defence Committee 'KOR', widening the scope of its activities and standing up in defence of all people persecuted for voicing their opinions and for acting in defence of law and order, democracy, freedom of speech and association in civic, religious, political or professional interests. 'KOR' supports independent social initiatives and exposes lawlessness (eg. murders in police custody unmasked in **A Book of Lawlessness**).

Since the first strikes in July 1980 we have gathered and published information about the strikes and workers' demands. We realized that the authorities can only use repression and suppress a strike when nobody knows about it. We knew that one plant's experiences can be of help to others. When on 18 August 1980 the region of the Baltic Coast on strike was cut off from the rest of the country, we spread information about the strike, about the formation of the Inter-Factory Strike Committee and its 21 demands to dozens of big enterprises.

On 20 August 1980 over a dozen of more active 'KOR' members and collaborators were arrested. It was not my first time in prison, this time a few days only, but altogether I have spent 6 years in prison. Now every additional day behind the bars is more difficult. It is obvious that I have very personal reasons for gratitude and I an turning to you now, when I am being slandered by every possible means in the press, radio and television. I am approaching 50. I have no position, no property, no titles, my only possession is my good name of which they are trying to deprive me. They resort to lies, forgery, and provocation and they have at their disposal the most sophisticated technical means, a powerful propaganda machinery, and large sums of money for bribes. You remember well that when the Inter-factory Strike Committee was formed it was said that it was the work of anti-socialist elements who had found their way into the ranks of the strikers; in inner circles it was said that 'KOR' was directing the Coastal strike action.

I do not know why the West German weekly **Der Spiegel** chose to publish this version of events. But I do know why the Polish press and television repeated it. Some were meant to believe that it was an anti-socialist plot, others to be angry with me for talking such nonsense. The authorities were also hoping that Lech Walesa — called a front-line lieutenant — would take offence. Ridiculous small-minded people. They do not know that only they want to become at all cost generals, secretaries and ministers. We: Lech, Anna, Andrzej, Bogdan, myself, we are all front-line officers. We are and always want to be in the first line of the struggle for human rights, workers rights, national rights. As a matter of fact they have somewhat promoted us, for an officer in the army gives orders, while we only can and want to listen to the people who are fighting together with us and for whom we are fighting, who believe us and who must control us.

There are many difficult tasks in front of us. Independent and self-governing trade unions will not by themselves bring about more meat in the shops, shorter queues, better transport, more flats. These and all other goods we need must be produced by a well-organized industry, agriculture, building trade. After many years of hard work we have learned that its fruits have been wasted, the situation is bad and will become worse. We cannot count on a good party secretary; we have to organize ourselves democratically and take the affairs of the country into our own hands. Yet full independence is impossible: we have to take into consideration the external forces guarding the leading role of the party in the state. We consciously give up a part of our independence and concentrate on the trade unions which will truly defend workers' rights, on self-government in industry, on farmers' organisations, and a genuine co-operative movement, on independent student movement and independence of research, culture and education. This is the meaning of the Gdansk agreement which is mainly your achievement. To fulfil this agreement, not to waste this great national opportunity, is our common task, the task of all Polish citizens who do not think only of their personal or group interest.

STATEMENT
Social Self-Defense Committee 'KOR'
Warsaw 15 November 1980

On 11 November 1980 after a patriotic demonstration to celebrate the 62nd anniversary of the regaining of independence, Wojciech Ziembinski of ROPCiO (Movement for the Defence of Human and Civil Rights) was detained. The District Prosecutor's Office Warszawa-Srodmiescie charges him on the basis of articles 270,273 of the Penal Code ('Whoever publicly reviles, derides, or degrades the Polish nation, the Polish People's Republic, her system or central authorities .. by means of print or other mass media') and article 276 of the Penal Code (on participation in an association with a view to committing a criminal act). These articles provide for a sentence of up to ten years in prison. Wojciech Ziembinski has been temporarily detained.

Wojciech Ziembinski has been fighting for national traditions, for setting in public view those elements of our national history which have contributed to the formation of the Polish nation and which have been passed over in silence, or even destroyed, by the authorities. Wojciech Ziembinski has been one of the organisers of solemn celebrations of national anniversaries, or of the commemorations of famous Poles. In recent times he fought for the reprieve of the Kowalczyk brothers, political prisoners sentenced to 25 years in jail.

On 12 November 1980 Zygmunt Galecki, an independent social activist, was temporarily arrested in Siedlce.

The Social Self-Defence Committee 'KOR' points out that Leszek Moczulski has been in jail since September, charged with political offences. The arrests of Wojciech Ziembinski and Zygmunt Galecki are particularly worrying as a symptom of a systematic campaign against independent social activists. It shows that political persecution has not ceased in our country. Repression on political grounds threatens the whole renewal movement developing now in Poland.

(The following is the full text of the Polish Prosecutor General's notes — the ones which were confiscated on 20 November during the search of Warsaw 'Solidarity' offices. This led to the arrest of Jan Narozniak, a Warsaw 'Solidarity' printer.

The document is prefaced by Warsaw 'Solidarity' statement of 1 November, and by a short statement by its chairperson, Zbigniew Bujak.

According to the Information Centre for Polish Affairs *the Polish original contains mistakes. For example, the Social Self-Defence*

Committee 'KOR' is called, the Social Solidarity *Committee 'KOR'; and people's names were mispelled. In addition Kuron and Modzelewski were sentenced for distributing a document 'harmful to the interests of Poland' and not for 'an attempt to overthrow the political system of Poland by force'; and the 'taterniks' were arrested, tried and convicted in 1969 and not in 1968.)*

STATEMENT
Presidium of NSZZ 'Solidarity'
Mazowsze region
Warsaw 21 November 1980

On 20 November 1980 at 4.30 p.m. security and police functionaries led by the Deputy Prosecutor Mrs W. Bardonowa, searched the headquarters of the NSZZ 'Solidarity'—Mazowsze region. During the search they confiscated a document on the subject of law and order in our country. The document is entitled: 'On the present methods of prosecution of illegal anti-socialist activity' and it was sent on 30 October 1980 by the Chief Prosecutor L. Czubinski to the institutions subordinate to him.

The document reveals many cases of arbitrary police decisions amounting to abuse of power and infringement of the law. Moreover, it takes them totally for granted, proving thereby that the Prosecutor's Office has been used as a tool by the security apparatus. The aim of the document is to show that the emergence of independent trade unions is a direct result of all 'anti-socialist' activity. This means that a large section of the judiciary has not accepted the Gdansk agreement. Under the circumstances it bodes ill that the Chief Prosecutor advises his subordinates to 'use skillfully the enclosed text in their political and professional work'.

On the day after the search of the union headquarters Jan Narozniak — a volunteer for union printing work — was summoned to the Ministry of Internal Affairs for questioning, and detained there.

We are warning the authorities not to return to repression. We demand the immediate release of Jan Narozniak. If he is detained any longer, we shall have to call a strike alert in selected enterprises of the Mazowsze region.

At the same time we demand that L. Czubinski's role in the violations of the law in the past decade be revealed, especially his responsibility for the persecution of workers in Ursus and Radom after June 1976.

Zbigniew Bujak

Chairman of the Mazowsze region Presidium of NSZZ 'Solidarity'

I hereby state that although I was not aware of the presence of the text in question on the premises of the Mazowsze 'Solidarity' union or of its duplication, had I known about it I would have ordered it to be duplicated in a number of copies sufficient to distribute to every circle of our union. This text poses a threat to the interests of NSZZ 'Solidarity'.

THE PROSECUTOR'S PLAN FOR A CRACKDOWN

I enclose a document "On the present methods of prosecution of illegal anti-socialist activity" to be used skillfully in political and professional work.

Lucjan Czubinski
Chief Prosector of the Polish People's Republic
Warsaw 30 October 1980

The activities of illegal anti-socialist groups, originating among the intelligentsia, began towards the end of the 1950s. They involved chiefly junior academics and students of Warsaw University, with the co-operation of a group of intellectuals in Krakow.

In their initial stage they took the form of discussion meetings of students and social gatherings with lectures on subjects of a political and economic nature, followed by debates which presented a distorted picture of the system of the PPR (Polish People's Republic) and other socialist states, detracted from their achievements and criticised the direction of their further development.

Towards the end of 1964, the Security Service, in the course of a search in the home of a member of the 'Warsaw Group', Stanislaw Gomulka, found a document called: 'A programme of the working class'.

Subsequent investigations have shown that it had been written chiefly by Karol Modzelewski and Jacek Kuron with the co-operation of Stanislaw Gomulka and Bernard Tejkowski.

A few months later, it was revealed that Mr Modzelewski and Mr Kuron had written an 'Open Letter' to the local group of the PUWP (Polish United Workers' Party) and members of the ZMS (Union of Socialist Youth) at Warsaw University. Both documents, which were clearly hostile to socialism, were largely devoted to an exposition of Trotskyist-revisionist ideas and, in fact, called for the overthrow of the system of the PPR by force.

It is highly significant that, among a number of revisionist recommendations, the 'programme' demanded the creation of trade unions that would be independent of the state, giving the working class the right to strike, and replacing the unified party of the working class with several parties competing with each other.

As a result, K. Modzelewski and J. Kuron were arrested, tried and convicted of an attempt to overthrow the system of the PPR by force. In separate proceedings Kazimierz Badowski, Ludwik Has and Romuald Smiech were arrested, tried and convicted on a similar charge.

At the same time a number of persons were prosecuted for contacts with centres of ideological diversion abroad, and supplying them with materials slandering the system and the authorities of the PPR.

In 1968, the following persons, among others, were arrested, tried and convicted of such charges: Maciej Kozlowski, Maria Tworkowska, Krzysztof Szymborski, Jakub Karpinski and Maria Szpakowska (so-called 'Taterniks'), all of Warsaw University.

In June and July 1970, there followed the arrest, trial and conivction of 30 members of an illegal political organisation 'Rukh' (Movement). In this organisation were assembled a number of educated people in Lodz, Warsaw and Lublin who had close connections with the clergy. The leaders were four brothers Czuma: Hubert, Lukasz, Andrzej and Benedykt.

Their programme was clearly anti-socialist. It favoured unlimited private property, denied the role of the working class as the driving force of the nation, and questioned the leading role of the workers' party. The activities of 'Rukh' consisted in working out and spreading an ideology hostile to socialism, later also in terrorist acts (the attempt to blow up the statue of Lenin in Poronin).

Apart from these most important activities of anti-socialist groups in the 1960s and 1970s, a number of other cases of hostile anti-socialist action were exposed. These were also dealt with by means of judicial reprisals (for example, the arrest, trial and conviction of Melchior Wankowicz, the arrest of Stanislaw Salmonowicz, and others).

In connection with the so called March events of 1968, and later with the so-called December events of 1970, as well as with the events of 1976 (at Ursus and Radom), similar judicial action was taken against persons guilty of offences against public order and social property.

The disturbances of 1976 in Radom and Ursus were followed by a considerable activisation of anti-socialist forces which embarked on large-scale action, including action involving violations of the criminal law.

In September 1976 there came into being an illegal association which called itself the Workers' Defence Committee (KOR), consisting of a number of people for years engaged in anti-socialist activities (J. Kuron, J. Litynski, A. Maciarewicz, A. Michnik, M. Mikolajska and others). This association (on 29 September 1977) transformed into the Committee of Social Solidarity (KOR), has since been engaged in activities, some of which have the character of criminal offences.

The increased activity of persons who, after the Radom-Ursus events, continued to stimulate social unrest which could result in further violations of public order (for example, there was an attempt to use the Juvenalia celebrations in Krakow as an occasion for disturbances by spreading false rumours on the causes of the death of the student Pyjas), made it necessary to start an investigation and to apply in May 1977 temporary arrest in the case of seven persons most actively engaged in criminal activities: Jacek Kuron, Adam Michnik, Antoni Maciarewicz, Piotr Naimski, Wojciech Ostrowski, Jan Jozef Lipski.

They were suspected of having organised, and of continuing, cooperation with foreign organisations hostile to Poland: Radio Free Europe, Institut Littéraire in Paris, 'Aneks' and others, against the political interests of the Polish People's Republic by means of feeding them specially concocted untrue information and papers on social and political conditions in Poland.

The investigation confirmed facts of conceiving, printing and distributing (also abroad) information containing often false news on, among others, reprisals against persons guilty of infringing the law.

Wide distribution of such news could have led to further disturbances of public order. However, investigations failed to supply adequate evidence of the existence of direct links of the people involved with hostile foreign organizations (Radio Free Europe, the journal *Kultura* in Paris). Preparatory proceedings against all those people were quashed on the basis of the amnesty decree of July 20, 1977.

The years 1977-1980 saw the further organizational strengthening of contestatory elements. Besides KSS-KOR, other organizations came into being, such as the Movement for the Defence of Human and Civi Rights, Students' Solidarity Committees, Peasants' Self-Defence Committees, the Movement of Young Poland, the Confederation for Independent Poland.

These organizations gained ever-wider influence by means, among others, of large-scale publishing and propaganda activities. About 30 periodical publications (newspapers, bulletins, magazines) were being edited, printed and distributed. A number of new brochures were published and several books were printed. A number of titles appeared in several thousand copies. Tens of thousands of leaflets were distributed, spreading the views and slogans of anti-socialist groups directed against the established authority.

These polygraphic and publishing activities were conducted without the approval of the Central Office for the Control of the Press, Publications and Performances (GUKPPiW), which is an offence against Art 6 of the Decree of August 5, 1946, which established the GUKPPiW.

It has been decided that the part of the aforesaid organizations in this illegal criminal publishing activity can be treated as an offence against Art 276, p 1 of the Criminal Code. It is also possible to invoke Art 273, p 3 of the Criminal Code in qualifying the activities of persons playing a leading part in KSS-KOR and other illegal organizations.

Regulations of the criminal law may also be useful in considering the contents of some papers, such as Leszek Moczulski's **Revolution without Revolution** which is, in fact, the programme of ROPCiO (the Movement for the Defence of Human and Civic Rights) aiming for the seizure of power (if need be with the use of force) by anti-socialist elements.

It must be emphasized that the author, in presenting his version of overthrowing the system in Poland, says that this will be preceded by a period of ever more solid and powerful organizational structures of political (anti-socialist) forces, of the expansion of the free press, local self-government and independent trade unions. In other words, it would be a period of constructing a power that would be able to take over the state.

It should be emphasized that in recent years methods of dealing with persons engaged in anti-socialist activities have changed. The idea of arranging criminal trials has been abandoned in favour of merely administrative preventive action to preserve order.

Types of actions undertaken by the Security Services in order to limit the extent of negative initiatives launched by organized anti-socialist groups, and to counter the creation and distribution of illegal publications, as well as isolating anti-socialist elements from their social and professional environment, were the following:
1. Numerous searches which brought to light large quantities of illegally produced publications destined for distribution, as well as of equipment for producing and stencilling them;
2. Sequestrating and withholding such items;
3. Detaining persons by the police in order to paralyse their anti-socialist activities;
4. Applications to tribunals for petty offences to punish persons who in the course of their anti-socialist activities commit petty offences.

The part of public prosecutors in these actions consisted in:
5. Approving searches and the sequestration of objects seized in the course of searches, as well as issuing in sporadic cases orders for searches to be carried out;
6. In several cases persons engaged in anti-socialist activites were sued in courts for ordinary crimes;
7. Twice — in December 1979 and in August 1980 — temporary detention fo several days was applied to groups of persons engaged in anti-socialist activities.

Ad 1: Searches are, strictly speaking, one of the main forms of counteracting the influence of anti-socialist elements on society exerted by means of illegal manufacture and distribution of propaganda. They are carried out by members of the Security Service (SB) and the police (MO), as a rule on orders by officers commanding SB and MO units.

Mostly these are searches in houses, but also personal searches (for example, of persons detained for distributing something). They are usually carried out in regard to persons engaged in anti-socialist activities. The results are almost always positive; witness the fact that, out of some 200 searches carried out in the second quarter of this year, only a few proved fruitless.

Ad 2: The searches yielded large quantities of various illegal publications, among them periodicals such as *Robotnik (The Worker), Glos, Biuletyn Informacyiny, Krytyka, Dziennik Polski, Zapis, Biuletyn Dolnoslaski*

(Bulletin of Lower Silesia), *Zeszyty Historyczne, Zeszyty Towerzystwa Kursow Naukowych* (Bulletins of the Society of Scientific Studies), *Gazeta Polska, Rzeczpospolita, PPN, Gospodarz, Aneks, Postep, Placowka, Bratniak* (Students organisation), *Uczen Polski* (Polish school pupil), *Robotnik Wybrzeza* (Sea Coast Worker).

The findings include books and brochures published illegally by the so-called Independent Publishing House, Nowa, as well as single publications, such as *Revoultion Without Revolution, On Trade With The West, Crisis or Breakthrough, The Authorities and the Opposition, Facing the Future, After the Great Leap, In the Middle of Life, Poisoned Humanities, Song of the Rebel, How Long Are We to Suffer, To All Working People, The Story of Katyn, The Black Book of Censorship in the PPR, Notes on the Hungarian Revolution* and others.

Other sequestrated findings consisted of large amounts of various leaflets, appeals and posters calling on people to protest against various moves of the authorities and to support anti-socialist activities.

Further, a certain amount of unauthorized literature from abroad, particularly publications of the Institut Littéraire in Paris. The number of copies seized varied from search to search, from single items to many hundreds. In the first quarter of this year a total of some 10,000 copies of various such publications have been seized.

The searches resulted also in the sequestration of a certain amount of equipment and materials for the manfucture of illegal publications — typewriters, duplicators, ink, paper, and others.

Ad 3: Detentions were usually effected in connexion with various meetings of leading members of anti-socialist organizations or "editorial boards" of illegal publications..Those detained were persons who stencilled, printed or distributed illegal publications, or who were in possession of such materials. They were detained in local police cells.

Members of the Security Service conducted, or tried to conduct with them conversations of an explanatory, conscience-forming character, mostly without any result.

As a rule, the detained were released within 48 hours. In exceptional cases, such as in August, 1980, the total period of detention of several persons exceeded the legal norm. Several leading activists of anti-socialist groups (Mr Kuron, Mr Michnik and others) were successively held in several police cells for 48 hours each time.

Complaints addressed to the public prosecutor are evidence that these persons were, in fact, freed within 48 hours, but on leaving the police station they were again arrested and held for the next 48 hours. The complaints are proof that between successive detentions the persons were allowed to have a walk, a cup of coffee at a bar, or to buy fruit.

Ad 4: In a number of cases people engaged in anti-socialist activities were pubished by Tribunals for Petty Offences. These were such offences as: illegal assembly (Code of Petty Offences, Art 51, p1), spreading leaflets (dropping litter in public places, Art 145), shouting sogans (Art 51, p2), illegal gathering in the street (Art 50 of the Criminal Code), wearing without permission a badge of the Confederation of Independent Poland (Art 61, p1, Code of Petty Offences).

Data supplied to the Prosecutor-General by the Investigation Bureau of the Ministry of the Interior, showed that the total of persons sentenced in this way in the second quarter of this year was 31. In most cases the sentence was a fine, in several cases imprisonment. Applications for punishment were issued by the local police station. In cases of appeal from the Tribunal for Petty Offences to a court, public prosecutors appeared in the appeal trial.

Ad 5: The part of public prosecutors in counteracting contestatory moves consisted, among others, in carrying out functions involved in the preparation of a trial. At the moment the Investigation Bureau and Investigation Departments of Regional Police Commands are in the course of carrying out, under the supervision of public prosecutors, preparatory procedures in 15 cases involving criminal activities of members of anti-socialist groups.

They are under way in the following localities: Warsaw (two cases), Gdansk, Lublin, Katowice, Cracow, Poznan, Torun, Radom, Szczecin, Wroclaw, Lodz, Rzeszow, Walbrzych and Kalisz. In such cases the prosecutors usually approved searches carried out by the police, as well as the sequestration of objects found in the course of these searches.

The basis of approval were the results of the searches in the form of publications issued and distributed by anti-socialist groups. The contents of these publications are usually judged in the light of Art 271 or 273 of the Criminal Code.

It must be emphasised that in cases where the content of the publication was unimpeachable from the point of view of criminal law, as a basis for approving a search and sequestration the fact was sufficient that the publication was the result of a crime of its having been printed without the consent of the Central Office for the Control of the Press, Publications and Performances.

The large number of sequestrated objects — typewriters, duplicators, paper, and above all illegal publications — in some cases creates problems of storage. It has, therefore, been decided, on the basis of Art 201, p1 of the Code of Criminal Procedure, to transfer the publications to the waste paper disposal unit.

Ad 6: Several persons engaged in anti-Socialist activities, who had committed common crimes, were brought to court for criminal trials. In the second quarter of this year nine such cases were initiated, and several of them resulted in convictions.

These were crimes committed in connection with anti-socialist activity, or unconnected with it. In the first group were such offences as stealing paper, a typewriter, a duplicator, or smuggling a duplicator into the country; in the second, beating or threatening to beat somebody, threatening to use a knife and conspiring to obtain a false statement.

Ad 7: In December, 1979, and towards the end of August this year, preparatory procedures current at the time involved temporary detention in the case of several most active oppositionists, because while at large and continuing their subversive activities they might have caused serious public disturbances (in December, 1979, in the Gdansk coastal area, in August this year in connexion with strikes throughout the country).

In December, 1979, in cases conducted under the supervision of public prosecutors in Warsaw and Lodz, 15 persons were detained. In August, 1980, 21 persons were detained in Warsaw, and seven in other cities — a total of 28 persons. They were arrested under Art 276 of the Criminal Code, that is, for crimes committed by virtue of being members of associations (KSS-KOR, ROPCiO) pursuing the criminal activity of producing and distributing various publications without permission from the GUKPPiW.

The basic evidence which justified the detentions of August 1980, consisted in the first place of large numbers of illegal socio-political and economic publications, seized in the course of searches carried out in the suspects' homes.

Information contained in these publications was desgiend to cause social unrest, it was tendentious, full of demagoguery, sometimes quite false, although not always falling under the specifications of Art 270, 271 or 273 of the Criminal Code. In all cases, however, it was published without the consent of the Central Office for the Control of the Press, Publications and Performances, and thus qualified as a crime under Art 6A of the Decree of August 5, 1946.

The character, quantity and contents of these publications as well as the methods of their production and distribution, were unequivocal evidence of an organized publishing activity carried out in the framework of the above-mentioned illegal political organizations.

Some publications even stated quite openly that they were issued by these organizations. Some articles were signed by persons who thereby admitted, as it were, their activities within these illegal organizations. The extent of the publication activities thus exposed and documented indicated that this, indeed, was one of the most important purposes of these organizations at the present stage.

All these facts were taken into consideration when detentions were ordered, as well as in the formulation of charges concerning the involvement of these persons in associations (illegal political organizations) formed for the purpose of committing a crime (publishing without the consent of the Central Office for the Control of the Press, Publications and Performances).

It must be said, however, that the evidence on which the detention orders were based was not sufficient and, if the investigations were to be completed, the indictment would have to be considerably enriched.

This will necessitate in the first place the acquisition of some personal evidence (explanations given by the suspects, depositions of witnesses) which would make it possible to assemble adequate proof of the guilt of the arrested persons. In view of the fact that persons involved in anti-socialist activities have in recent years adopted the tactics of refusing, as a rule, to make any statements in the course of the preparatory procedure, the task of acquiring such personal evidence encounters considerable dif-ficuties.

It is absolutely necessary to pay much more attention to the problem of documenting much more extensively than in the past the effects of the criminal activities of anti-socialist groups.

At present, deeds of persons taking part in anti-socialist activities are treated as participation in an association whose purpose is to produce and distribute illegal publications (offences under Art 276 of the Criminal Code). However, some actions of these groups go beyond the specification of this regulation.

From some articles and public statements of members of anti-socialist groups, it is clear that they also envisage the possibility, even the need, to take over power in the state, even by force. Nowadays they declare this quite openly.

Preparations for the implementation of such ideas could serve as grounds for qualifying this activity from the point of view of criminal law as action preparatory to, or even initiating, the overthrow of the system established in Poland. Therefore, in securing more extensive evidence account should be taken of the need of selecting and recording evidence that would permit also the formulation of such charges.

General Public Prosecutor's Office, Departments II and III
Warsaw, October, 1980.

ix TOWARDS WORKERS' SELF-MANAGEMENT

We publish here one of the very few texts that has reached us from Poland from outside official circles which is putting forward a general political plan for change. The article was part of a collection of discussion documents produced inside the Warsaw Area organisation of Solidarity. It puts forward a radically democratic and indeed socialist perspective for change.

As yet the government hasn't even put forward a programme of short-term reforms, dealing with the dramatic economic situation, and aimed at stabilising our communal life. We cannot passively wait for a government programme of action. The situation demands immediate and decisive action. It is working people, above all else, who are interested in the reformation of the Polish People's Republic, and indeed only they are capable of carrying out the necessary reforms.

In Poland a struggle is being waged for a self-managing society. The outcome of the struggle, and with it the future of our country, will depend on whether it results in the creation of new institutions, which will allow society to decide for itself, and give it sovereignty over economic and political matters.

It is particularly important to develop a broad-ranging discussion in the workers' movement about the necessary economic and institutional reforms. They must concretise our visions of a self-managing society. We must not allow a situation in which, yet again, laws (dealing with trade unions, censorship, self-government, the workplaces) are handed down 'from above' by a committee of experts. We cannot entrust the perspectives for the development of the country to anyone but working people as a whole.

The initiation of such a discussion demands in the first place complete information about the socio-economic situation. The trade union press must have reports on the state of various areas of the economy and the general standard of living, along with concrete proposals for change. More information about economic initiatives is needed. This is already being undertaken by workers in various parts of the country. The work of the Council of Planning needs to be developed by regional councils and by the Committee of the Agreement; they should work out a complete programme of socio-economic reforms and prepare it for public discussion.

Below we try to map out the most urgent points, which such a reform programme should take into consideration. We will concentrate above all on the problem of basic institutional changes.

1. The Tasks of the Independent Trade Unions.

The aim of the solidarity strike action during the summer was, above all else, to win the right to independent workers' self-organisation. This would become the institutional guarantee that the interests of the working masses in Poland would never again be taken lightly. If 'Solidarity' is to fulfil this aspiration it cannot restrict itself to the defence of the economic interests of the workers; it must also defend their interests as producers. If the free trade unions restrict their activities to the sphere of economic interests, this will inevitably lead to competition between different groups of workers, which would tear our movement apart from the inside. The consequences of such competition would be the strengthening of the government's apparatus; when faced with sectoral interests it would come out in the role of a mediator, putting forward its own interests as the interests of society as a whole.

Maintaining solidarity among working people and strengthening their organisation creates the possibility of taking up the struggle for participation in all decision-making about important social and economic matters. The maintenance of this solidarity is also the precondition for the creation of authentic organs of self-management, able to control the administration of each workplace, region and the whole country.

2. Workers' Self-management

The organisational structures of 'Solidarity' have enabled it to weather internal fractures and particularism, maintained among the workers until now by the old trade unions (which were organised along trade lines). The present structures have not only ensured the unity of the workers in the country as a whole (the token strike on October proved this) but also allow the creation of organs of workers' self-management at the head of each factory, region and finally throughout the whole country.

Workers' self-management at factory level must include the whole workforce. Equipped with the necessary methods of decision-making and control, it should decide about production and social matters in the factory as a whole. At the same time it must control the implementation of these decisions by the management and administration. In particular, it must be able to decide about vacancies in the management.

In many factories the genesis of authentic workers' self-management can be seen. The free trade union must take up the matter of production because, quite frankly, many factories are run incompetently.

Today nobody but the workers themselves can ensure that the efforts of the workforce do not go to waste. On top of this, in many factories management is engaging in economic sabotage. It lowers production figures, disorganises production and industrial co-operation with the aim of placing the blame for poor production figures on the free trade unions.

3. The Workplace.

The functioning of workers' self-management, of which we spoke above, is determined by the autonomy of the workplaces, resting on the process of local planning. The self-management of the workforce will be illusory unless it is confirmed by the economic autonomy of the factories. In this regard, the problems of self-management become directly tied to the question of radical changes in the method of drawing up the central, sectoral and factory plans, along with the complete reform of the economic system. In this context, the question of inspectors' evaluation of the factories must be integrated (the results of the Hungarian economic reforms are unusually instructive).

4. Agriculture

Self-management of the PGR's, the rebirth of authentic co-operation and above all else the self-management of the peasantry are among the most pressing problems, if we're not only thinking of institutional reforms but a strategy which will take us out of the economic crisis.

The August turning point, slogans of independence and solidarity must be taken as quickly as possible out to the countryside; to the peasants.

Agriculture, ignored in discussions till now, treated instrumentally and without greater recognition in relation to all the problems of the countryside, must become a central subject of the work on planning.

Even now, significant sectors of the productive forces must be given over to the manufacture of tools and materials necessary for agricultural production, even at the cost of sectors of industry dealing with consumption. This is something we must do now — for the benefit of the most effective sectors of industry. It is necessary to combat dogmatism on this issue. It is effectiveness which decides, and not formal labels (PGRs or private enterprise). This means dogmatism of all kinds; the one formal, the other stemming from a lack of recognition of the real agricultural situation. This is why it is necessary to develop and strengthen all forms of self-management in agriculture. While placing the emphasis on the self-management of the peasantry, one must not forget about the hundreds of milliards frozen in the state sector. This capital must be used. No one will do this without the self-management of agricultural workers.

5. Sejm (Parliament)

Workers' self-management will not be in a position to carry out its role and put pressure on the administration, until the links between individual workplaces lead to coordination of their activities on a regional scale, and regional self-management coordinates its activities on a national scale. Such co-ordination was lacking in 1956 between the Workers' Councils which had been set up at the time. Today we must draw the lessons of that experience.

Only the Sejm, as the highest organ of legislative and executive authority, can assure the necessary coordination of regional organs of self-management.

In its present form, the Sejm represents a society which no longer exists; a society which has been destroyed, atomised and which is capable of being manipulated by the authorities. 1980 has seen the rising of a new society in Poland, which is organised, and wants and is able to defend its rights and sovereignty. The Sejm has, up till now, acted as a Parliamentary facade for the authoritarian rulers. At the time of the August strikes, as the fate of our country hung in the balance, the Sejm remained silent. Today, in spite of many attempts to overturn its constitutional role, the most important decisions regarding our society are taken outside of it. Now the Sejm agrees with the irresponsible attitude of the authorities towards 'Solidarity' (the affair of the registration), and doesn't protest about interference in Poland's internal affairs of foreign powers. It is significant that such a protest wasn't made by the deputies, but by 40,000 members of 'Solidarity' in the Lenin Steelworks.

The Polish parliamentary system needs to be fundamentally reformed. The millions of workers organised 'below' must demand real representation 'above'. The entry of representatives of the free trade unions into the Sejm must be seen as a top priority. New elections to the Sejm and the National Councils, with new electoral regulations, must be called as soon as possible. The new regulations ought to guarantee the right of the free trade unions to propose their candidates for a Workers' Bench, which must be created in the Sejm, if this institution is to recover the attributes of representation and credibility.

The reform of the Sejm is important, above all else, because the implementation of socio-economic reforms requires the passing of a series of laws dealing with the new forms of society. The parliamentary road is the lackey's road. This we must remember. That is why the trade unions must take part in the preparation and enactment of these laws.

The entry into the Sejm of representatives of the free trade unions does not in the slightest mean that the trade unions want to play the role of a political party, and take up the struggle with the Polish United Workers' Party for state power. It is necessary so that the party stops the pretence that it fulfils (albeit in the name of the Constitution) the role of arbiter, independent of the Constitution, placing itself above the Sejm and above any control by society. It cannot play its leading role in the country only on the basis of a constitutional clause and control of the repressive apparatus. It must earn the right in real life, in democratic elections and in the Sejm. It cannot, as it has till now, impose its programme on society in an administrative manner; it can only realise it through the activity of its members in the trade unions, local government and other institutions of self-management. Today there stands an independent trade union movement opposing the party, and the link between these two camps is the mass of party members, especially in the big industrial workplaces. The ability of the party to reform itself and join in the movement which started in August, depends on their determination, attitude and action. But this cannot be on the old terms of direction and domination, but to serve.

TOWARDS SELF-MANAGEMENT

—By W. Wypych and H. Szlajfer

X LINKING UP WITH SOLIDARITY

(The following is a list of the main workplaces, divided up in regions, which are affiliated to the new trade unions, NSZZ Solidarity, and who can be contacted for 'twinning/direct links' projects. This list has been established in each case after contact with official representatives of MKZ — local and regional inter-workplace committees.)

GDANSK REGION

MKZ: Hotel Morski, Grundwaldska 103, Gdansk. Tel: 41.95.26/41.62.34/41.11.11
Stocznie im. Lenina (shipyards): Gdansk.
Stocznia Polnocna (shipyards): Ul. Poskiej 177, Gdansk.
Stocznia Remontowa (shipyards): Ostrow. Na Ostrowiu, Gdansk.
Stocznia Gdynskia Komunii Pariskiej (shipyards): Ul. Czechoslowacka 3, Gdynia.
Port Gdynski (Port): Gdynia.
Rafineria NAFTY (chemical industry, refinery): Ul. Elblaska 135, Gdansk.
Gdanskie Zaklady Nawozow Fosforowych (chemical industry, refinery): Kanal Kaszubski, Kujawska 2, Gdansk.
UNIMOR (electronics, TV, radio): Gdanskie Zaklady Elektroniczne, Ul. Rzeznicka 54/56, Gdansk.
RADMOR (electronics): Gdynia
Urzad Telekomunikacyjny (telecommunications): Ul. Lutego 10, Gdynia.
PKP (railways): Polnocne DOKP Gdansk, Ul. Dyrekcyjna 3, Gdansk.
Wojewodski Zespol Przeciwgruzlicki (hospital): Ul. Partyzantow 21, Gdansk.
Portowy Zespol Opieki Zdrowotnej (hospital): Ul. Chrzanowskiego 3/5 Gdansk.
WPK (transport): Ul. Jaskowa Dolina, Gdansk-Wrzeszcz.
University: Al. Bazynskiego 1a, Gdansk.
University: U. Czerwony Armii, Sopot.

WARSAW REGION

MKZ: Ul. Szpitalna 5, Warsaw. Tel: 27.74.33/27.44.81
URSUS (tractors): Ul. Traktorzystow 1, Warsaw-Ursus.
FSO (motor-cars): (FIAT Polski), Al. Stalingradzka 50, Warsaw.
TEWA (electronics): Ul. Komarowa 5, Warsaw.
ZWAR (radio equipment): Ul. Zeganska 1, Warsaw.
MERA PNEFAL (electronics): Ul. Poezji 19, Warsaw.
Zaklady Mechaniczne im. M.Nowotki (precision tools): Fort-Wola, Warsaw.

POLFA (chemical industry): Biuro Porjektow Przemyslu Farmaceutycznego, Ul. Zurawia 6/12, Warsaw.
MZK (urban transport): Miejskie Zaklady Komunikacy, Ul. Senatorska 37, Warsaw.
PKP (railways): Polski Koleju Panstwowy Ziemi Mazowieckej, Dworzec Centralny, Warsaw-Centre.
Huta-Warszawa (steelworks): Ul. Kasprowicza 132, Warsaw.
WPT (post and telecommunications): Warszawa Przedsieborstwo Telekomunikacjnych, Ul. Zabraniecka 8, Warsaw.
Bank PKO (bank): SA III Oddzial, Ul. Traugutta 7/9, Warsaw.
Zespol Opieki Zdrowotnej (hospital complex): Szczesliwicka 36, Warsaw-Ochota.
Muzeum Narodowe (museum): Al. Jerozolimskie 3, Warsaw.
UNITRA-POLKOLOR (colour television factory): Zaklady Kineskopowe, ul. Matuszewska 14, Warsaw.

KRAKOW REGION

MKZ: Ul. Karmelicka 16, Krakow, tel: 249.97.
HUTA IM. LENINA (steelworks): Krakow.
Elektrownia Skawina (electrical energy): Skawina.
UNITRA TELPOP (electronics): Centrum Naukowa Produkzyjne, Ul. Lipowa 4, Krakow.
MERA—KWAP (electronics): Fabryka Aparatow Pomiarowych, Ul. Elektryczna 6, Tarnow.
Fabryk Maszyn Odlewniczych (metal industry): Ul. Cystersow, Krakow.
Fabryka Obrabiadek Specjalinowanych (machines): Andrychow.
POLLENA (Chemical industry): Fabryka Kosmetykow, Ul. Zablocie 23, Krakow.
Debickie Zaklady Opon Samochodowych (chemical industry): Ul. 1-go Maya 1, Debica.
Zaklady Azotow (chemical industry): Tarnow.
Drukarnia Wydawnicza (printing): Ul. Wadowicka 8, Krakow.
Instytut Inkologniczny (medical institute): Ul. Garncarska 11, Krakow.
RABKA (hospital): Zespol Opieki Zdrowotnej, Ul. Sloneczna 3, Nowy Sacz.
MPK (urban transport): Miejskie Przedsieborstwo Komunikacijne, Ul. Wawrzynca 13/3, Krakow.
PKS (urban transport, buses): Krakow.
WISTULA (textiles): Zaklady Przemyslu Odziezowego, Ul. Nadwislanska 13, Krakow.
Akademia Gornicza Hutnicza (academy of technical sciences): Ul. Mickiewicza 30, Krakow.
Akademia Ekonomiczna (academy of economic sciences): Ul. Rakowicka 27, Krakow.
Jagiellonski University: Krakow.
Krakow Polytechnic: Ul. Warszawska 24, Krakow.

LUBLIN REGION

MKZ: Okopowa 7, Lublin.
FSC (motor-cars): im. B. Bieruta, Ul. Melgiewska 7/9, Lublin.
WSK (metal industry, engines): Swidnik
Fabryka Lozysk Tomcznych (tyre factory): Krasnik
Cukrownie 'Lublin' (sugar refinery): Ul. Krochmalna 13, Lublin.
Elektrownia (electricity): Kozienice
Okregovy Urzad Telekomunikacijny (telecommunications): Ul. Staszica 14 a, Lublin.
Narodowy Bank Polski (bank): Chopina 6, Lublin.
Domy Towarowa 'Centrum' (trade): Kralowskie Przedmiejsce 40, Lublin.
Muzeum Okregowe 'Zamek' (museum): Zamkowa 9, Lublin.
Drzewo Chemiczna Spolzielna Inwalidow (invalid cooperative working in the chemical industry): Do Dysa 4, Lublin.
Catholic University of Lublin: Ul. Raclawickie 14, Lublin.
Academy of Medicine: Cicha 4, Lublin.
Zaklady Azatowy (chemical industry): Pulawy, Lublin.
Zespol Opieki Zdrowotnej (hospital): Ul. Staszica 22, Lublin.
Okregowo Przedsieborstwo Przemyslu Miesnego (foodstuffs, meat): Krasnik
Rozglosnia (television and radio): Bozy Dar, Lublin.

KATOWICE REGION

MKZ: Dabrowa Gornicza, Katowice,
tel: 68.150.
Kopalnia Wegla Brunalnego (coal mines): Belhalow
Fabryka Obrabiarek Ciezkich Poreba (machinery): Zawiercie.
Wezel PKP (railways): Tarnowskie Gory
KBO (housebuilding): Sosnowiec
Fabryka Obuwia 'CHELMEK' (footwear): Bedzin
Wojewodstwo Przedsieborstwo Handlu Wewnetrznego (trade, shops): Katowice.
Zespol Opieky Zdrowotnej (hospital): Dabrowa Gornicza.
Wszystkie Biura Projektow 'BIPROCHOL' (projects institute): Glinic.

WROCLAW REGION

MKZ: Plac Czerwony 1/3/5, tel: 55.55.11., Wroclaw.
PAFAWAG (railway compartments): Fabryka wagonow, Ul. Pstrowskiego, Wroclaw.
DOLMEL (electric generators): Ul. Pstrowskiego, Wroclaw.
ELWRO (electronic computers): Ul. Ostrowskiego, Wroclaw.
POLAR (refrigerator factory): Ul. Zimierskego, Wroclaw.
HUTA LEGNICA (copper mines): Legnica.

HUTMEN (smelting works): Ul. Grabiszynska 241, Wroclaw.
Diora Dzierzoniow (electronics, radio): Wroclaw.
Jelczanskie Zaklady Przemyslu Samochodowego (Berliet lorry factory): Olana.
ARCHIMEDES (chemical industry): Ul. Robotnicza, Wroclaw.
CHEMITEX (chemical industry): Ul. Kwidzinska, Wroclaw.
CHEMIZOLA (chemical industry): Ul. Traktatowa, Wroclaw.
Hospital: Plac 1-go Maya, Wroclaw.
OTIS (clothing): Ul. Traugutta, Wroclaw.
CUPRUM (copper industry administration attached to Lublin mine): Plac 1-go Maya, Wroclaw.
WSS-SPOLEM (trade, shops): Wroclaw
Stocznia Rzeczna (shipyards): Wroclaw.

PLEASE NOTE: To contact the workers of these workplaces, it is necessary to address them as: Solidarnosc NSZZ Committee.

LIST OF SOLIDARITY CONTACTS

Gdansk
Alina Pienkowska, Ul. Tylewskiego 30, Gdansk-Suchonino.
Anna Walentynowicz, Grundwaldska 49/m, 9 Gdansk.
Gdansk MKZ: Ul. Grundwaldska 103, 80-244 Gdansk, Tel: 41 11 11; 41 62 34; 41 95 26.

Huta Katowice
Andrzej Rozplochowski, Ul. Czerwoniych Sztandarow 94/ m 115, 401-303 Dabrowa Gornicza.

Jastrzebie Zdroj
Jaroslaw Sienkewicz, MKZ Zastrzebie, Ul. 1 Maja 32, Tel: 62074.

Walbrzych
Zbigniew Kocik, Ul. Lenin A 8/1, 58 — 304 Walbrzych.
Stanislaw Wrobel, Ul. Hutnicza 9, 58 - 300 Walbrzych.
Walbrzych MKZ: Ul. Wysockiego 23, Walbrzych, Tel: 22 810.

Wroclaw
Andrzej Blaszczyk, Ul. Gajowa 56 m.14, 50-520 Wroclaw.

Lublin
Zdislaw Szpakowski, Ul. Szopena 35, Lublin.

xi IN RETROSPECT

Some silly or irresponsible people in the West have gone along with the Soviet view that the August strikes were created and manipulated by a handful of activists. Such fantasies of the police mind should not, however, obscure the important role in the field of ideas played by the unofficial trade union activists during the two years before the strikes of this summer. Especially important here was the role of the workers' journal Robotnik **which appeared regularly from the autumn of 1977 onwards. And in the summer of 1979 on the initiative of** Robotnik **a Charter of Workers' Rights was drawn up and signed by activists from all over Poland. We reproduce this document below and readers will be struck by the emphasis given in the text to the struggle for the right to strike and to the right to create independent trade unions.**

The document was first published in Labour Focus **Vol.3 No.4. September-October 1979.**

THE CHARTER OF WORKERS' RIGHTS

Whereas:
— citizens are being deprived of the right to take part in decision-making on matters that concern them;
— restrictions are being imposed on the fundamental rights of the employee such as the right to safe and pensionable work, to a just wage, and to rest
— social inequalities and injustices are becoming more profound;
— there exist no institutions to protect the employee — the official Polish Trade Unions are not institutions of this kind;
— workers are denied their fundamental right of defence, which is the right to strike;
— society has to shoulder the cost of every mistake of the authorities, including the cost of the current crisis;

we have entered upon a course of action whose long-term aim is the creation of a self-defence system for employees, first and foremost, independent Trade Unions.

We wish to begin with the problems which seem to us to be capable of solution, at least in part, at the present time.

1. WAGES

— pay should rise at least in step with the cost of living; a **cost of living** supplement is essential;
— everyone should be ensured a **minimum living wage**; teams of

specialists should work out this minimum and amend it in proportion to rising prices; families living below this line should be paid appropriate supplements;
— efforts must be made to eliminate glaring and unfounded differences in pay;
— stoppages of work, changes of quota, etc., must not be allowed to entail a drop in wages;
— workers doing the same job under the same conditions should receive remuneration in accordance with standardised scales of rates which are independent of the branch in which the said workers are employed.

2. WORKING HOURS

— it is inadmissible that overtime, additional and community work should be compulsory; miners must have Sundays and holidays free;
— the **free Saturdays** of the current system must be legally guaranteed to everyone;
—efforts must be made to implement a **40-hour working week without reduction of wages.**

3. OCCUPATIONAL SAFETY

— safety standards and regulations must be observed **without exception**; there should be special commissions to monitor this, having wide powers including the right to shut down a plant; commissions monitoring occupational health and safety, accident commissions and also factory doctors must be institutionally independent of the factory management;
— no one who suffers loss of health due to harmful working conditions can be left without the pay or income to which he is entitled;
— it is essential to update the current list of industrial diseases;
— **night work for women** must be eliminated; it should not be allowed that women do heavy physical work.

4. GRANTING OF PRIVILEGES

— the remuneration of an employee and his promotion should not depend on his party allegiance, political opinions nor outlook;
—benefits such as bonus payments, housing or vacations must be allotted in an open manner; the means of allotting these goods and the names of the beneficiaries must be openly announced;
— there must be an end to the granting of privileges to groups connected with the government (police, party functionaries): special allowances of goods greatly in demand, such as housing, plots of land, building materials, cars, special medical care, luxury holiday homes, special pension rights, etc.

5. COMPULSION TO ACT AGAINST ONE'S CONSCIENCE

— no one should be forced to immoral acts, to inform for the Party

or the security service, to take part in attacks on undesirable persons;
— people should not be compelled to produce shoddy goods, to carry out work which threatens their safety and that of others, to hush up accidents, make false reports, etc.

LABOUR CODE

The Labour Code in force since 1975 must be radically changed. It established regulations which are disadvantageous to the workers. Its articles are equivocal, and hence in any given situation can be and frequently are interpreted to the benefit of the management. In particular:

— Article 52 must be changed. It is used as an anti-strike law (the numerous sackings after June 1976 were based on it); the right to strike must be **guaranteed by law**;
— if someone is dismissed, the management must explain in writing the reason for the dismissal; the worker should continue in his job so long as his case is going through the successive legal instances; throughout the whole process he should have the right to the assistance of a lawyer;
— union officials elected by the work force must be legally protected against dismissal for a certain time after laying down office also.

We consider that the realisation of these postulates depends on our own stance. Evidence that workers can force the authorities and management to make concessions is provided by the great showdowns of 1956, 1970 and 1976, and by individual strikes. For several months now, we have felt the effects of the crisis on our own skin. Deliveries and transport get worse and worse, wages are going down, prices are going up, in big plants the working hours are getting longer and are taking up the 'free Saturdays', there are more and more stoppages. If we ourselves do not now make a start at defending our own interests, our situation will go from bad to worse.

However, in order to win, we must rid ourselves of any feeling of impotence, stop passively putting up with restrictions on our rights and the deterioration of the conditions of life, and must look for the most effective form of action. There exist a great number of possibilities.

A. Undoubtedly the most effective form of action is to strike, even if the strikes are not on a large scale. Generally however, it is only effective in the short run. In order not to waste the achievements of a strike, the participants must elect representatives to monitor the realisation of their demands. If the workers know how to act in solidarity and are not afraid, they can force management to concessions by the very threat of a strike, by presenting petitions, or sending delegations.

B. A very great deal can be achieved simply by the dissemination of information. It is necessary to speak up loudly and to protest when someone is wronged, when we see injustice; it is necessary to publicise the actions of cliques and the granting of privileges, shortcomings, and wastage, breaches of the regulations on occupational health and safety and the hushing-up of accidents. It is necessary to speak about this to colleagues and at meetings. To demand that the authorities take a stand on this. To tell the independent social institutions and the independent press.

C. There are many problems in labour relations which can be solved by using the official trade unions. It would certainly be better for us if these were not so dead as in fact they are at present. We must demand that the factory councils defend the interests of the workers, we must use union meetings for discussions and put forward demands to them, and must elect to factory councils people who will realise the demands.

D. A condition for our actions to be something more than ad hoc and haphazard is the existence of a group of workers in a state of constant alertness. This group, even if implicitly at first, can draw up a programme of activity, organise a series of actions, form public opinion, and, in time, come out into the open as independent workers' committees.

E. Wherever there exist strong organised communities of workers who are able to defend their representatives against dismissal from work and imprisonment, free trade union committees should be set up. The experience of employees in the Western democracies shows that this is the most effective way of defending the workers' interests.

Only independent trade unions, having support among the workers whom they represent, have any chance of opposing the authorities. Only they will represent a force with which the authorities must reckon and with which they can deal on equal terms.

We, the undersigned, pledge ourselves to work towards the postulates contained in the Charter of Workers' Rights.

We are also setting up an Aid Fund and pledge constant contributions to it. The resources collected in the Fund will be used to assist persons dismissed from work for taking part in independent union activity.

xii AN AFTERWORD TO THE NORTH AMERICAN EDITION

One of the greatest events of the Twentieth Century is unfolding in Poland. What the world is witnessing in that country, which has been divided, dominated and decimated for generations by various imperial powers, is the flowering of courage and hope, not for the support of nationalism, but in the service of humanity.

These are grand words and they come hesitantly, however the documents published herein testify to the fact that the people of Poland are attempting nothing less than to take full control of their modern industrial society. The means they intend to use is Solidarity. And Solidarity, clearly, is not simply an anti-Soviet trade union, but the working people of Poland mobilized for the extension of true democracy to all economic and cultural institutions.

The reverberations of the movement have already crumbled the old party structures, and next, also long over due for demolition, will be the industrial hierarchy that has sequestered the creative potential of the workers. The local chapters of Solidarity have been busy for months circulating bulletins discussing the pre-conditions for workers' self-management and its implications for the economy and society.

These discussions (which Ztangi Press will be publishing) have a special relevance to those in other modern societies that find themselves victimized by the industrial complex that they built but do not control.

Unfortunately, the world is inhospitable to social experiments that benefit ordinary working people and so Poland faces difficult times ahead. There are three centers of power, all international in scope, that can effectively side-track this noble undertaking, if not crush it altogether. The Roman Catholic Church is probably the least likely to curb the tide of Polish will, though many in the West, so accustomed to the machinations of a sclerotic, bourgeois Church find it difficult to appreciate that a more liberal element exists. Nonetheless the Church in Poland has for so long accomodated the power structure one justifiably wonders if it can easily adapt to new circumstances. And of course it remains as hierarchical now as before August. We have still to see a movement develop for a priests' union!

The second unknown force in Polish affairs is the Soviet Union. The possibility of an invasion has been analyzed so extensively in all the media that the pros and cons of such a move must be as familiar to the average American as to the Kremlin. On the whole an invasion seems more improbably if avenues of dialogue remain open with the Soviet Union, and on this score, with a reactionary regime in Washington drumming up war hysteria, the prospects of such a dialogue depend upon Western European countries. More precisely, our hope rests on a mass, direct action movement for disarmament in both West and East Europe.

The third force involved in Poland, and the most likely to have its way is world capital. Poland owes approximately $24 billion to the West, and only $8 billion of this is guaranteed by various governments. Sixteen billion is outstanding to Western commercial banks, of which one-third is due to West German banks. If Poland defaults on these debts, not only would it seriously disrupt the Western banking system, but also Comecon, the Soviet bloc economic unit. The pressures from world capital are bound to be subtle, they will certainly never make the headlines or the evening news, and for that reason they are all that more pernicious. We shall know that capital has regained its dominance when the excuses for bureaucracy and regimentation came flying again from the Polish borders.

In sum, the best way to help the Polish workers achieve the freedom that they strive for is to recognize that their fight is our fight. The dominance of world capital is felt as cruelly in Poznan as in Pittsburgh. The only way to end this nightmare, which we may never survive, is to realize that our struggles are the same, that we must learn from one another, and that with practical expressions of international solidarity we shall attain the free society we all desire.

Bernard Marszalek
May, 1981

GLOSSARY

Commercial Prices: After the successful strikes against food price increases in June 1976, the government set up special 'Commercial Shops' charging higher, so-called 'commercial' prices alongside the normal outlets whose prices remained frozen. The entire strike movement this summer began in response to an unannounced shift of various kinds of meat from the normal outlets into the commercial shops exclusively, thus effectively raising prices by over 30%.

Confederation for Polish Independence: a Nationalist group on the right of the political spectrum, led by journalist Leszek Moczulski, who has been held in jail since September. The Confederation was created in autumn 1979. For more information on it see **Labour Focus** Vol.3 No.4(Sept.1979).

CFDT: The second largest French trade union federation loosely associated with the French Socialist Party.

DIP: A reformist-oriented group that emerged out of a commission involving party and non-party intellectuals set up by party leader Stefan Olszowski. When the group's discussions were given publicity in the West in December 1978 some of the party members, who included **Polityka** editor Rakowski, withdrew from formal membership of the group.

Edmund Zadrozynski and the Kozlowski brothers: for more information see pages **61** and **76** of this issue.

Gomulka's October 1956 Speech: In 1956 a mass, popular upsurge linked to a reformist current inside the Communist Party, brought Gomulka to power as Party leader. He had been the Communist Party's general secretary during the war and during the first post-war years, before being expelled from the party and jailed as a supposed enemy of socialism at the end of the 1940s. Gomulka came to power in October 1956 despite strong Soviet hostility. He threatened resistance if the Kremlin tried to use force and spoke out for respect for national independence within the East European region. Gomulka was replaced by Gierek after ordering the shooting down of protesting workers on the Baltic following his decision to raise food prices in December 1970.

Information Bulletin of KSS-KOR: The initials stand for the 'Social Self-Defense Committee — Workers Defense Committee'. This, the main opposition group, was formed in September 1976 as the Workers' Defense Committee to campaign for the release of workers jailed after the June 1976 strikes that prevented the government raising food prices by about 64%. The following summer, when the campaign had successfully gained the release of all the jailed workers, the KOR broadened its aim to encouraging various social groups to speak up against harassment against them by the state.

The KSS-Kor Information Bulletin has been appearing since 1976 as a thick duplicated magazine packed with information and comments on events in Poland. The membership of KOR itself has been only about a couple of dozen but it is the inspiration of many other committees and journals not formally linked to it. Its members are not homogenous and do not consider their committee to be a 'political party' but most of them are drawn from the lay, socialist wing of the Polish intelligentsia; their coming together as an open committee reflected a trend within the non-Catholic intelligentsia away from any perspective of encouraging a reformist faction in the Communist Party and towards a new co-operation with sections of the Polish Catholic Church.

Nomenklatura: This is an extremely important mechanism of power in all East European countries, deriving from Soviet practice. The word refers to the list of jobs in society which various Communist Party Committees have the right to fill with people of their own choice. Top national jobs are within the jurisdiction of the Central Committee and local jobs are within the jurisdiction of the regional party committee. The lists of jobs are kept secret. The nomenklatura system means that, for example, the top posts in the official trade unions were simply filled by the Central Committee with people of no previous qualifications or experience in the trade unions whatever. This system is 'the leading role of the party' in practice.

Our Lady of Czestochowa: also known as the 'Black Madonna', it is a painting of the Virgin Mary kept in the Monastery of Jasna Gora near the town of Czestochowa. Legend has it that the painting demonstrated miraculous powers, intervening to defeat the Swedes in a battle in the area in the 17th Century. The Monastery is now the most important shrine for religious pilgrimage in Poland.

PAP: The official Polish Press Agency.

PKS: These initials stand for the Paris Commune Shipyards in Gdynia.

PUWP: The initials of the official name of the Polish Communist Party — the Polish United Workers' Party. This name comes from December 1948 when the Polish Socialists, under enormous pressure from Moscow, fused with Poland's Communists to create a single party.

Robotnik and Placowka: Robotnik (The Worker) is the name of an independent trade union journal that began in the autumn of 1977 and before the August crisis this year had a print run of about 20,000. It played an extremely important role in gathering together unofficial trade unionist activists from all over the country in one common network, exchanging experiences and ideas on the problems of the workers' day to day struggles. **Robotnik** popularised the need for independent trade unions and other key demands raised by the mass of workers during the August strikes. **Placowka** is an independent journal of the peasants.

Szydlak: appointed head of the Central Council of Trade Unions in February this year and sacked during the August crisis, one of Gierek's longest-standing lieutenants. He spoke very violently against the Gdansk strikers before being removed from the scene by them. He had had no previous trade union experience before being appointed head of the unions.

The Appeal of the Intellectuals: It was signed by some of the most distinguished contemporary intellectuals from Poland's official culture, including many members of the Academy of Sciences. We could mention former leading Party ideologist W. Bienkowski, writer Marian Brandys, historian W. Kula and many others.

The National Unity Front: an organization that appears at election times. It unites the Communist Party, its two satellite parties and various social organizations all presenting a common, single list of candidates in the elections.

The Three Cities: This refers to the neighboring cities of Gdansk, Gdynia and Sopot now linked together as one economic and social unit.

8th Party Congress: The most recent one, in February 1980.

Voivodship: The regional administrative unit of the Polish State. There are now 49 such areas.

MAP OF POLAND